TEACHING WITH CHILDREN'S LITERATURE

Also Available

Principles of Effective Literacy Instruction,
Grades K–5
Edited by Seth A. Parsons and Margaret Vaughn

Teaching with CHILDREN'S LITERATURE

THEORY TO PRACTICE

Margaret Vaughn
Dixie D. Massey

Foreword by Elfrieda H. Hiebert

THE GUILFORD PRESS
New York   London

Library of Congress Cataloging-in-Publication Data

Names: Vaughn, Margaret, author. | Massey, Dixie D., author. | Hiebert, Elfrieda H.,
    author of foreword.
Title: Teaching with children's literature : theory to practice / Margaret Vaughn,
    Dixie D. Massey ; foreword by Elfrieda H. Hiebert.
Description: New York : The Guilford Press, 2021. | Includes bibliographical references
    and index.
Identifiers: LCCN 2021021489 | ISBN 9781462547227 (paperback) |
    ISBN 9781462547234 (hardcover)
Subjects: LCSH: Children's literature—Study and teaching. | Children—Books and
    reading. | BISAC: EDUCATION / Teaching Methods & Materials / Language Arts |
    LANGUAGE ARTS & DISCIPLINES / Literacy
Classification: LCC PN1008.8 .V38 2021 | DDC 809/.89282—dc23
LC record available at *https://lccn.loc.gov/2021021489*

About the Authors

Margaret Vaughn, PhD, is Associate Professor of Literacy in the College of Education at Washington State University. A former first-grade teacher, she conducts research on adaptive and equitable practices to support student agency and literacy learning. Dr. Vaughn is coeditor of *Principles of Effective Literacy Instruction, Grades K–5*. Her work has appeared in many journals of literacy research and practice.

Dixie D. Massey, PhD, is a lecturer at Seattle Pacific University, where she teaches courses in literacy development and teacher preparation. Dr. Massey is coauthor of several curriculum books and series. She has published her research in leading journals of literacy research and practice.

Foreword

Resilience means you don't have a fit when you don't get
what you want, and you don't give up easily.
—SUZANNE,[1] a second grader, at a meeting of her
(virtual) Nancy Drew book club

There are just too many strange words in my books. I want to
go back to preschool. We didn't have homework in preschool.
—LOUISE, a first grader, during a virtual tutoring session

Underlying these two statements are different views of agency—the capacity to
make choices and follow through with appropriate actions—and the role of reading and books in supporting choices and actions. For Suzanne, books are sources
of messages that transfer to and even transform your life. For Louise, books are
to be avoided. In *Teaching with Children's Literature: Theory to Practice*, Vaughn and
Massey address what we rarely discuss with our students: the underlying beliefs
that readers and teachers have about reading and its role in our lives.

Literature is fundamental to supporting students in building agency as
learners. Suzanne may well have begun reading the Nancy Drew books with
a firm growth mindset in place. Even so, her experience in reading about an
intrepid young woman has strengthened that mindset by giving her an example
of what it means to confront challenging situations with resilience. For Louise,
who approaches the task of reading with apprehension, purposeful teaching is
essential—and soon! It is unlikely that a year in second grade that mirrors her
first-grade experience—absent of literature and conversations about students'
roles as readers—will change her trajectory to that of an engaged reader.

What can teachers do? The purchase of a set of leveled books or trade books
doesn't guarantee that teachers have books at their fingertips that will develop

---

[1] Student names are pseudonyms.

their students' agency. Nor can we assume that a read-aloud of a highly acclaimed book will support student agency. Throughout *Teaching with Children's Literature,* Vaughn and Massey underscore the need for teachers to have a deep and wide knowledge of both literature and their students in order to cultivate knowledgeable and strategic readers. But knowledge of literature alone is insufficient; this knowledge must be accompanied by beliefs and intentions that create and sustain purposeful reading opportunities throughout not just a school day but the school year.

Teaching with Children's Literature came into my life at the right time—while I was tutoring Louise virtually during the sheltering in place precipitated by COVID-19. After hearing both of the statements that introduce this foreword in the same week, I couldn't help but contrast Suzanne's perspective with that of Louise. How might I draw on some of the recommendations in this book to ensure that Louise becomes a reader who benefits from the power of literacy?

Before outlining the actions that I've drawn from this book to apply to my tutoring, I should note that as I write this foreword, the tutoring is still in its early stages. As a result, I can't conclusively describe the shifts in Louise's view of herself as a reader. I can tell you, however, that the benefits go beyond Louise: my own agency as Louise's tutor has increased substantially, and as I communicate my actions to Louise's parents and suggest ways that they can extend them, they, too, are more encouraged.

Addressing my beliefs and intentions, as Vaughn and Massey suggest throughout the book, was a first step in increasing the purpose and power of the instructional sessions. My first action, then, has been to stop focusing our tutoring sessions on a set of instructional books that I believed, based on my assessments of her oral reading fluency and word recognition, were a perfect match for Louise. I haven't stopped using the books entirely, but I have stopped making them the focus of our sessions. Making this change has been no minor feat. After all, I had written these instructional books myself, and they had been proven successful in research studies! But it became clear to me that I needed to refrain from limiting Louise's reading to a specific genre of texts.

Instead, I initiated a second action, which has been to select a set of high-quality books, both for read-alouds and for Louise's independent reading. I have long been an advocate of outstanding literature as the foundation for classroom-based English language arts experiences. But since I recognized that Louise has not gotten off to a great start as a first grader, the message looping through my mind has been "If we don't cover this today, Louise could be in trouble for a long time to come." My beliefs (really, my fears) have blocked my awareness of the foundational role of outstanding literature in developing a habit of lifelong reading. As I read *Teaching with Children's Literature,* I was able to step back and recognize the futility of ensuring technical competence in reading without fostering a love for reading.

One way to learn to love reading is to find ourselves in what we read. Now the books that I've chosen for Louise all have primary characters who bear a sufficient resemblance to her in appearance and disposition. Several books by Ashley Spires in which female protagonists take on challenging tasks seem especially germane. I predict that *Fairy Science* (Spires, 2019) will be a particular hit because Louise is a great fan of fairies.

As a result of Vaughn and Massey's guidance—especially in the chapters on encouraging students to read widely and in contexts beyond the classroom—I have included book series in my recommendations for Louise. I admit that I had to be persuaded to include these texts. As a literacy educator, I haven't always been enthusiastic about the amount of school time that American students spend with series such as *The Wimpy Kid*—a series that is, according to *What Kids Are Reading*, number one in grades 4 and 5 (Renaissance Learning, Inc., 2020). In general, I have nothing against book series, and, under duress, I confess to being a fan myself of certain mystery series. But shouldn't students be reading at least some great literature? Again, reading *Teaching with Children's Literature* nudged me into confronting my beliefs: Vaughn and Massey make a strong case for recognizing students' choices. And so I found a series in which the first book's title alone—*Uni the Unicon*—excited Louise (Rosenthal, 2014).

My final action has been to place the texts for instruction and the follow-up sessions into a knowledge framework. No, I haven't eliminated the little instructional books from our tutoring. But I have done considerable reshuffling of the books based on two types of knowledge: (1) knowledge about the world and (2) knowledge about words. A recurring theme of *Teaching with Children's Literature* is that literature is a source of knowledge about our personal, social, and physical worlds. As Vaughn and Massey remind us, the funds of knowledge that students have gained in their homes and communities provide a foundation for their future learning. At the same time, literature is a means for extending existing bodies of knowledge and gaining new ones.

Knowledge about words and how words work is also critical in becoming an engaged and proficient reader. As a literacy educator, I know that independent reading is grounded in the automatic recognition of words. This automaticity is based on guidance highlighting the similarities and uniqueness of words, followed by opportunities to apply and generalize these insights. By organizing instructional texts by topic and by key linguistic features, students have the chance to see specific words and patterns repeated. One topic that Louise knows a great deal about (and I don't) is cats; Willow, her family cat, has been a faithful companion during the many days at home. She finds the topic engaging and, in pursuing information that interests her, she is adding to her knowledge about pets, as well as becoming more fluent as a reader.

Although it's still too early to gauge my success as a tutor, *Teaching with Children's Literature* has been a source of hope and insight to me in this role. I know that Vaughn and Massey's book will offer others—teacher educators, teachers, and parents—guidance and support as they themselves serve as guides to students navigating new terrain.

Elfrieda H. Hiebert, PhD, *TextProject*

REFERENCES

Renaissance Learning, Inc. (2020). *What kids are reading*. Wisconsin Rapids, WI: Author.
Rosenthal, A. K. (2014). *Uni the unicorn*. New York: Random House Books for Young Readers.
Spires, A. (2019). *Fairy science*. New York: Crown Books for Young Readers.

Contents

CHAPTER 1

Introduction

BELIEFS ABOUT CHILDREN'S LITERATURE

Welcome to *Teaching with Children's Literature: Theory to Practice*. We wrote this book to help preservice teachers, practicing teachers, teacher-educators, and other educational stakeholders use children's literature to develop purposeful reading opportunities in today's schools. We discuss the relevant theories about this topic and ways to translate these theories into instructional practices. We emphasize three main components in this book: teachers must develop knowledge of their students, knowledge of instructional practice, and knowledge of literature in order to use children's literature effectively in the classroom. The overriding goal of this book is developed around the question, How can we create purposeful reading opportunities in today's schools?

Our view is that purposeful reading opportunities are centered on the belief that *students have agency as readers in and out of the classroom*. We see agentic readers as readers who have the intentions, the knowledge, and the abilities to expand opportunities in their world and to use reading as a tool to accomplish this goal. A central understanding of cultivating agentic readers is that teachers construct purposeful reading opportunities in which students can engage meaningfully with literature.

- *Intentions*. When we talk about developing students who have intentions, we mean that students have a variety of linguistic and cultural backgrounds as well as life experiences. The goal of helping students realize that their intentions are valid is based on the ideas that reading is free, that it has no limits or boundaries, and that students can read anything that interests them. Teachers must capitalize on their students' backgrounds, interests, and topics they want to pursue when it comes to developing reading opportunities.

- *Knowledge.* Just as intentions are necessary when developing agentic readers, so is knowledge. Developing instructional opportunities based on creating knowledgeable and skilled readers is paramount. Agentic readers are active readers who are able to interpret, analyze, and critique a multitude of texts for a variety of purposes.
- *Ability to expand and transform.* As readers have intentions and knowledge, they can use reading as a tool to expand their horizons and to transform the world around them. Agentic readers can take a critical approach to what they read and use the knowledge gained from texts to expand opportunities.

Teachers are essential in cultivating agentic readers. They must integrate their own beliefs, knowledge, and targeted instructional practices to make decisions that support learning environments that are conducive to reading. Providing this kind of environment calls for teachers who are purposeful in teaching, consider students' identities and interests, adapt curricula, and possess a vision of teaching. Essential in this process is for teachers to continue their own learning trajectories to develop knowledge of their students, of teaching practices, and of literature.

WHY CHILDREN'S LITERATURE MATTERS MORE NOW THAN EVER

Children's literature matters now more than ever for two reasons. First, high-stakes accountability measures have resulted in narrowed curricula, which means students aren't necessarily able to read engaging, authentic, and culturally relevant texts. Second, we have greater diversity in our classrooms than at any other time in U.S. history.

Narrowed Curricula

The last three decades have seen an exponential growth in federal and state oversight of all education curricula, but especially in reading. The Reading Excellence Act of 1998 (REA; U.S. Department of Education, 2002), a landmark federal bill, provided competitive grants to states to improve reading instruction and to develop reading skills in students by using "scientifically based reading research," that included a systematic approach to reading instruction. Specific, targeted programs deemed as scientifically based were made available for states to purchase for reading instruction as a provision of receiving federal funds. The passing of the No Child Left Behind Act of 2001 (NCLB, 2002) federalized reading policies and the ways in which reading instruction filtered to classrooms across the nation (Allington & Cunningham, 2015). Accordingly, federal officials and their respective agents were in the new federally supported position of selecting particular instructional approaches, curricula, and assessment tools to be used to deliver reading instruction (Cuban, 2013).

The NCLB legislation of 2001 had a significant impact on the types of texts that were used in classrooms and on the reading opportunities made available to students. Proponents of the NCLB emphasized the need for a more systematic approach to supporting students when it came to reading instruction, especially those from the most vulnerable groups in the nation. Punitive measures were put into place for schools that did not meet their adequate yearly progress (AYP) goal. As a result, schools had to meet their AYP goal in order to receive funding or face corrective measures, such as replacing staff members, incorporating another scientifically based reading program, or offering the option to parents of enrolling their children in other schools and supplemental educational services to students. Critics of the NCLB pointed to the lack of culturally responsive texts and a focus on prescriptive reading instruction that emphasized a "one-size-fits-all" approach to developing student skills in reading. Ultimately, this direction widened the achievement gap for students from nondominant cultures and economically disadvantaged homes. These restrictive measures had a significant impact on the types of texts and the structure of literacy instruction in schools across the United States. Teachers were pressured to follow a prescribed curriculum and a uniform teaching approach to reading and literacy instruction. However, a one-size-fits-all program fails to meet the individual linguistic, cultural, and specific instructional needs of all students.

More recently, the Common Core State Standards (CCSS; National Governors Association Center for Best Practices & Council of Chief State School Officers [NGA & CCSSO], 2010) were adopted by 41 states (at the time of writing this book). A renewed emphasis on reading literature and especially informational text gained heightened attention in schools where the CCSS were adopted. Even so, children are not reading as much as they should at school. Allington (2012) estimated that for students to maintain their reading level, they need to read at least 90 minutes per day. Brenner and Hiebert (2010) found, on average, that students spent between 10.2 minutes and 24.4 minutes reading during reading instruction. Such findings suggest that the amount of time students spend reading within district-mandated literacy programs varies and can be as minimal as 10 minutes within a 120-minute block of targeted literacy instruction.

Unfortunately, even during sanctioned reading time in schools, curricula are restricted to materials that may or may not align with students' cultural, historical, or linguistic backgrounds. In fact, Brenner and Hiebert (2010) emphasized, "the amount of reading that is recommended in the instructional plans of these programs is not changing the trajectory of the very students for whom the mandates have been put in place" (p. 361). Simultaneously, when students are reading, they are not reading books of their choosing. Gambrell (2015) noted that in a recent survey of reading habits of children ages 6–17, only 33% reported that their class had a specific time during the day devoted to reading a book of their choice.

More Diverse Student Population

At the same time that teachers are coping with educational reform efforts and the resulting narrowed curricula, school populations are becoming increasingly diverse. Some researchers predict that students from nondominant backgrounds will constitute the majority of high school graduates in the United States by 2025. Diversity isn't only found in racial and ethnic categories. Consider a recent illustration of this broad diversity in the classroom:

> To illustrate what this means at the classroom level, an educator in the 1970s or 1980s with a classroom of 24 students might have had five or six students (20–34%) requiring specialized interventions. In a classroom of 24 students today, between 10 and 12 students (40–50%) are living in poverty, have a disability or learning difference, are English language learners, are gifted or talented, are experiencing challenges at home or in their communities that result in trauma, or some combination of the above—each of whom research shows needs personalized approaches to learning. (*https://digitalpromise.org*)

We argue that we need more books in the classroom, specifically those in which a wide range of characters are represented, so that all students, particularly students of color and from nondominant backgrounds, see themselves in the books they read and are afforded multiple opportunities to better understand a range of perspectives, (Beers & Probst, 2017; Mendoza, Kirshner, & Gutiérrez, 2018).

Some curricula include books that might appear to reflect diverse perspectives but whose content has not been carefully reviewed. We know of one fifth-grade teacher in a school with a large percentage of Native American students who was required to use the text *Voyage of the Half Moon* (West, 1995) as part of the required adopted state literacy program. This text portrayed and positioned Native American students as "these people" and "devils" (West, 1995, pp. 2–3; Vaughn, Parsons, & Massey, 2020). Our friend, Sonia, was outraged; however, she decided to use the book in a way that aligned with her beliefs and vision for teaching. She adapted the text to teach a lesson on social justice and had her students critically examine and rewrite the narrative using culturally responsive texts and historical records. Sonia was skilled at adapting her instruction and purposefully teaching to support her learners. Our concern is that these curricula are being adopted by school districts all across the country before the types of texts that students are recommended to read are carefully examined.

INSPIRING HOPE THROUGH CHILDREN'S LITERATURE

When students and teachers left their classrooms in mid-March 2020, none of them realized that they would not return anytime soon. A pandemic and social upheaval left many of us concerned for our physical safety and health. Our students felt the weight of many changes in their academic, social, and family lives, and in many other ways.

Using literature as a tool to read and respond to challenging and critical issues is widely documented in literacy research (Dutro, 2008; Koltz & Kersten-Parrish, 2020; Rodriguez & Kim, 2018). Teachers can use literature to share stories about how to process traumatic experiences (DÁvila et al., 2019; Wiseman, 2013); pose questions about their lives (Wee, Park, & Choi, 2015); and provide a way for students to express their own emotions and understand their experiences (Phillips & Sturm, 2013; Sipe, 2000; Wiseman, Atkinson, & Vehabovic, 2019).

Bibliotherapy uses books to build hope. Lucas, Teixeira, Soares, and Oliveira (2019) found that bibliotherapy was effective in instilling hopeful thinking. Similarly, Selin and Graube (2017) used book clubs with children in a children's hospital, and found that they helped generate hope as well as a sense of community with others who were enjoying the same books.

Hope is an area of specific research in multiple fields, including mental health, war and violence, trauma, and terminal illness. Valerie Maholmes (2014) has examined the role of hope during her tenure as the chief of the Pediatric Trauma and Critical Illness Branch at the Eunice Kennedy Shriver National Institute of Child Health and Human Development (NICHD). Maholmes described hope as the ability to envision a more positive future, even when all evidence points to the contrary, noting that hope is the most important predictor of success (Lahey, 2015). Hope is a "galvanizer of action" (Lazarus, 1999, p. 666) and can lead students to "engage in better problem-focused coping, greater agency in the face of negative feedback, more abundant pathways to solving problems when blocked, higher sense of well-being and, importantly, seeking more challenging goals" (Bullough & Hall-Kenyon, 2011, p. 130).

In our own research with teachers and students, we have found an important role for literature as a means of instilling a sense of hope, of engaging students in reading for enjoyment, and of helping them make connections to concepts and ideas that may otherwise be elusive. For example, in our research with fifth graders of the book *Paperboy* by Vince Vawter (2014), a young boy made a connection with a character who had a speech impediment and shared that he never read a book like this one in which someone had a stutter like him (Vaughn & Massey, 2017).

In short, the need to use literature as a tool to inspire hope and to foster agency is greater now than ever. Within the current educational context, and due to wider educational trends in curriculum and accountability, teachers have been pressured to narrow the materials that students read in the classroom. It is possible, even probable, that some students will only encounter short excerpts of texts and repeated test preparation materials and rarely be asked to read complete novels or nonfiction books. For example, in classrooms that we visit, we routinely see teachers using worksheets about novels to develop isolated skills, rather than providing students with the entire texts to read and enjoy and pairing the reading with focused and intentional discussion. This narrowing has occurred even while our classrooms have grown more diverse. Navigating this complexity requires teachers who teach with purpose.

TEACHING WITH PURPOSE: CLARIFYING CORE BELIEFS

We will spend more time in Chapter 2 exploring purposeful teaching. Here, we want to emphasize the importance of teachers' beliefs in relation to purposeful teaching. Taken together, beliefs and visioning are essential in developing knowledge about children's literature and in understanding how to apply this knowledge to instructional practices.

Beliefs shape what we pay attention to and thus what we learn. Teachers' beliefs influence the goals we establish for students, the procedures, the instructional content, and the interactions with texts. Beliefs affect how teachers see students and influence the type of instructional decisions we make and how we use assessments. They are the outcomes of past and present experiences and hoped-for futures. Beliefs do more than help us interpret our past and shape our present experiences; they can also guide our future actions. In this way, beliefs are frequently linked to action and how decisions are made about texts.

Before we became teachers, we had specific beliefs about teaching. These beliefs were strongly shaped by our own educational experiences (Darling-Hammond & Bransford, 2005). They influenced our learning when they pushed us to look for pedagogies that differed from what we experienced or that confirmed our way of learning. As we entered our teacher-preparation programs, we encountered new ideas in our methods courses. We rejected or assimilated these into our beliefs. We also encountered students who were different from us and experienced schooling differently than we did, and we again revised our beliefs.

Developing a belief system about children's literature as a teacher of children's literature can be a daunting task for many teachers, especially if reading is not something they normally like to do or they had negative experiences with reading in school. However, if we want our students to read, we need to critically reflect on our own experiences with reading, our preferences toward genres, and our beliefs about reading.

What do we know about the types of teacher beliefs that result in classrooms where children engage with literature in meaningful ways? The following beliefs about students and reading are essential when developing a classroom culture where students have agency.

Beliefs about Texts

What counts as text? What is the role of text in the classroom? These questions are critical to articulating beliefs about texts and integrating these beliefs into purposeful teaching.

Professional knowledge offers some direction in answering what counts as text. Recently, the International Literacy Association (2017) issued an updated definition of literacy. In addition to including reading, writing, speaking, and listening, this definition of literacy now includes viewing and visual representation. Practically speaking, looking at or creating a drawing with the intention to communicate are now viewed as literate behaviors. Have you ever watched a movie and found yourself connecting with the characters? Making a prediction about what would happen next? Drawing an inference about what motivated a certain action? Those processes are some of the same sense-making processes that we use when making sense of a text. It should be noted that this broad view of literacy is not always reflected in the curricula that teachers are given but one that we believe encompasses what literacy means today for all students. Moreover, text itself can be interpreted broadly—from digital platforms to various types of genres and formats.

What is the role of text in the classroom? Again, we look beyond what is typically handed down in curricula to see what researchers, professional educators, and students have said about the role of texts in the classroom. What all three groups have suggested is that texts, specifically authentic texts rather than text excerpts, are students' conduit to engagement with literacy tasks and with one another. In these texts, students note that they see themselves or begin to understand the points of views of others.

Furthermore, students want choice in the types of texts they want to read. The practice of providing choice in using children's literature includes offering opportunities for students to develop their interests, select and discuss books and provide other options for them to display their understandings.

Consider the following two classroom scenarios. Ms. Keen structures her classroom to include opportunities for students to self-select texts of interest and to pursue reading as a means of finding answers to questions students want to pursue. Ms. Gill uses a reward system in which students must attain a certain number of points per week in the computer-based reading program in order to attend the class party.

Which classroom do you think encourages students' agency toward reading, Ms. Keen's or Ms. Gill's? In Ms. Keen's classroom, she relies on building students' intrinsic motivation toward reading and encouraging her students to read regardless of whether or not they receive any reward. Students in this class learn that reading is something they can enjoy and use to develop their interests. In Ms. Gill's class, reading is tied to an extrinsic reward system wherein it's more than likely that most of her students will disengage and decide that reading is not for them if they can't accrue the number of points set forth by Ms. Gill to attend the party. In this class, students have limited agency. Providing opportunities for students to choose a wide variety of texts for multiple purposes is essential in developing a classroom culture supportive of reading in which students have agency as readers.

Beliefs about Tasks

What should we ask students to do with the texts we use? This question forms the core belief about reading tasks. One task we often observe in schools is an emphasis on reading rate. Students are frequently assessed on how quickly they can read a text out loud. We have observed school districts that emphasize this task from the end of kindergarten through middle school. Teachers use this reading rate as a benchmark for students' primary success in reading. Although reading rate is important, reading for understanding or comprehending is equally essential. Interpreting how and what we read influences and informs the way we develop skills beyond reading rate.

A different task is sense making of text. This goes beyond simply repeating information from the text and encourages students to engage with the text, apply their understandings of the text to their lives, and converse with others about the text. To encourage sense making, a teacher might opt to hold a discussion about a component of text or arrange a student-chosen book club so that students can talk with one another about the broader meanings of a text and how they understand it.

Using children's literature to develop authentic tasks is an important dimension of classroom practice. Teachers can structure tasks to create real-world and authentic learning opportunities that engage students with reading. Brophy (1983) described how the types of instructional tasks influenced students' motivation to learn. Academic tasks that were thoughtful and engaging encouraged students to value the process of learning and were considered to be the most beneficial in supporting students' willingness to participate and engage in the learning process.

Let's revisit Ms. Keen's and Ms. Gill's classrooms. In Ms. Keen's classroom, students choose reading materials to learn more about topics of interest to them and decide what to do with the knowledge they've gained. Some students create a poster about the knowledge they've learned, and other students decide to write a play to perform for the class. Students in this classroom make connections to their lives and personal interests and see that reading can serve as a bridge from their existing knowledge to future knowledge. In contrast, in Ms. Gill's classroom, students have little autonomy regarding the types of reading opportunities. The reading reward program she uses does allow students to choose the texts they read, but is restrictive because they can read only texts whose predetermined reading level matches their own reading level. The types

of texts students are able to choose shapes how they view themselves in relation to reading. It is important that teachers structure tasks in which students
approach reading as a tool that connects to their backgrounds, interests, passions, and questions they want to pursue—and not just as an exercise in reading
at a predetermined level.

Beliefs about Readers

What do kids deserve as readers? This question embodies the foundational beliefs
about readers. For a time in our past, children were viewed as tabula rasa—blank
slates to be filled. Although our society seems to recognize a particular set of
acceptable answers (e.g., kids are amazing, talented, capable, and unique individuals), our practices don't always match those beliefs. Instead, our practices,
such as curricula that require every student to read the same text for several days
of the week and complete the same set of questions, suggest that students are not
treated as individuals.

We further ask, who gets to decide what our students do with their texts and
tasks? In this book, we use a sociocultural framework. By *sociocultural*, we mean
that we emphasize the importance of students' home languages, background
experiences, and the ways in which they interact in relation to the world. According to Johnston and Costello (2005), "although we often think of literacy as a set
of all-purpose skills and strategies to be learned, it is more complex, more local,
more personal, and more social than that. Becoming literate involves developing
strong reading identities, relationships, dispositions, and values these as much as
acquiring strategies and skills for working with print. Children becoming literate
are being apprenticed into ways of living with people as much as with symbols"
(p. 256).

In a sociocultural framework, students' voices about their reading decisions
matter. Asking students questions about what they want to read and why they
want to read is a cornerstone of effective literacy instruction. This means that
students might choose books that are outside a recommended reading level for
them, but by giving them choice we offer them the opportunities to try, believ-
ing that they may surprise us and that there are multiple ways to engage with a
text. This is not to say that there aren't targeted instructional times during the
day when the teacher directs text selection for specific purposes, but that there is
allotted time for student choice and decision making in reading. Including and
highlighting students' voices in classroom discussions allow for them to become
part of a community and helps to create meaningful interactions that support
goals and identities. Becoming part of a community requires that students be
engaged in the learning process. Reading and engaging with literature are not
just mental activities but social and interactive opportunities. Reading literature
needs to be viewed in its full range of contexts—not just cognitive, but social and
cultural as well (Gee, 2012).

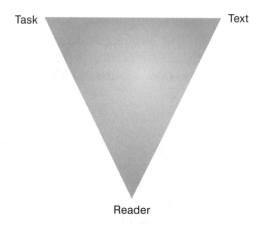

FIGURE 1.1. The reader–task–text relationship.

In sum, our beliefs and texts, tasks, and readers shape our choices about how we teach. Our conception of purposeful teaching connects beliefs to a larger sociocultural framework that views teaching and reading as a social, dynamic practice.

As Figure 1.1 indicates, the *reader* is the fulcrum on which everything is balanced. In other words, the teacher focuses instructional opportunities on the reader. The task and the text must be tied to and centered on the reader. Everything is guided by the reader.

PRACTICAL CONSIDERATIONS: WHO ARE WE?

We are former classroom teachers, and now teacher-educators and literacy researchers. We have been struck by the lack of reading we have observed in schools over the last several years. The literature says that kids aren't spending enough time reading during literacy instruction (Brenner & Hiebert, 2010) and lack opportunities to read engaging and authentic materials (Madda, Griffo, Pearson, & Raphael, 2011).

Unfortunately, reading authentic and engaging texts has been relegated to the background during literacy instruction, indeed an unfortunate situation we encounter daily in our work in schools. Students lack agency when it comes to reading. We continue to ask what might happen if we provide structures and supports in schools that cultivate and support agentic readers. We believe that children's literature is one of the most important components needed to refocus efforts to support reading in schools and to develop agentic readers.

This book explores the beliefs and knowledge teachers construct about children's literature in an effort to increase purposeful reading opportunities in schools and develop agentic readers. We emphasize the importance of developing visions inclusive of all students with regard to reading and the importance of having core beliefs about teaching with and understanding children's literature. We explore how teachers can come to know about children's literature by developing content knowledge about children's literature and the important theories that undergird what and how to use children's literature in the classroom. We want this book to be an important resource in developing practice-oriented knowledge, or knowledge of how to use theories and apply them to practice.

This book is organized into 10 chapters that feature a section on theories about the teaching of reading and practical considerations with a connected practice section. The theory and classroom practice sections include relevant examples and writing activities for readers. Each practice section contains questions for reflection, which are intended as ways for you to share your thoughts with a learning community or group or to track your thoughts in a learning journal. Each practice section also includes a case study that shows what theory in practice looks like in an actual classroom with an actual teacher.

PRACTICE

Cultivating agentic readers relies on incorporating purposeful reading opportunities in classrooms where students can engage meaningfully with literature. Because today's teachers face the challenge of narrowed curricular mandates and other uncertainties, we believe the need to support and cultivate agentic readers is greater now than ever before.

ACTIVITY 1. *Reflecting on the Reading*

1. When you were a student, what were your reading experiences? How was reading structured for you in elementary, middle, and high school? What were the positive and negative experiences? What types of books and materials were emphasized as part of reading in your schooling experiences? What types of reading materials do you like to read now?

2. When you think about these formative experiences, how have they shaped how you use (or hope to use) literature in the classroom?

ACTIVITY 2. *Examining Your Beliefs*

1. What do you believe is important about texts, tasks, and reading?

2. Create your own list of Beliefs about Reading that you can share with your students. Have your students complete their own Beliefs about Reading list. Talk together about your shared beliefs and develop classroom beliefs about reading.

Questions to consider when writing your own Beliefs about Reading:

a. What do you think is important when it comes to reading? I think that _____ is important when it comes to reading because. . . .

b. What types of books do you think are important to read? Why?

c. What do you believe should motivate students when it comes to reading? Why?

Questions to consider when asking your students to create their Beliefs about Reading:

a. What do you think is important when it comes to reading? I think that _____ is important when it comes to reading.

b. What types of books do you think are important to read? Why?

c. What do you believe will make you want to read? Why?

Questions to consider when creating the classroom's Beliefs about Reading:

a. What do we value when it comes to reading?

b. What types of books are valued in this classroom?

c. What do we believe will encourage us to want to read in this classroom?

ACTIVITY 3. *Case Study*

Read the case study of Jason in Box 1.1, which describes a real teacher's reflection about navigating his first year of teaching. Reflect on the questions about how his beliefs shaped his instruction.

1. List Jason's beliefs in the following areas: teaching, learning, students, and literacy.

2. How did Jason's beliefs influence his instruction?

3. What were the areas of conflict for Jason between outside expectations and his own beliefs? How did he respond to these conflicts?

ACTIVITY 4. *Using Children's Literature: What Do You Do with an Idea?*

Consider how texts can be used to empower and support student agency. Use read-alouds to model for students how to have agency with their ideas and how to use reading as a tool to act on their ideas. A powerful text that can be used to model agency for students is *What Do You Do with an Idea?* (Yamada, 2013).

Begin by asking students to generate ideas about topics and projects they would like to pursue. Using students' ideas, organize your class into groups with similar ideas and projects. Work with students to teach them how to research

BOX I.I. Jason: A First-Year Teacher Navigates Mandates and Expectations

As a first-year teacher in a middle school special education classroom, Jason admitted he was overwhelmed. He was frustrated with the literacy curriculum (worksheets, computer lessons, and regular Accelerated Reader tests) and frustrated further by the lack of motivation he saw in his students. Jason believed he couldn't change everything about the program immediately because he still had to work with the other team members who were very traditional in their approaches. He also knew that he had to be realistic about the planning time it would take to completely change the curriculum.

Jason hoped to emphasize the enjoyment of reading, not instead of learning necessary skills, but as an accompaniment to learning them. He felt that the heavily structured tasks were "coma inducing" for both the students and himself and were limiting student engagement. Jason reflected:

> "I want to be able to teach comprehension without feeling like a robot every time I intentionally try to do so. I want my students to feel successful, so that they can get past their insecurities with reading. I want the students to be engaged in the material and for them to not even know that they are learning. I want the students to have more time to just sink into a book and get lost amidst their day."

Jason decided to make two changes to his curriculum based on his beliefs and his vision for teaching: introduce reading for enjoyment and increase student reading time. His first specific change was to begin reading aloud to students at the beginning of each period, beginning with Kwame Alexander's (2014) *The Crossover*. Additionally, he allowed students a short amount of personal reading time each day. He did not quiz them on what they read but simply allowed them time to read in his class from a book of their choice. This change was not supported by the other resource room teachers, so Jason and Dixie, the second author, had ongoing conversations about this practice, with Jason asking, "Should I feel guilty about just letting them read?" His students responded positively, looking forward to hearing more from the read-aloud books and the books that others shared. They even reminded Jason if he neglected reading aloud to them.

Gradually, Jason began asking his students to talk with each other about what they'd been reading, and commented on what he learned:

> "I have been reluctant to talk about what books the students are reading in my sixth-grade class. There is so much disparity in their reading levels that I have been avoiding the potential for some students to shame other

(continued)

students based on their 'low' books and to further stifle progress. Today I decided to go for it, so I asked if anyone had a book that they were reading that they wanted to recommend to their reading community. Just as I feared, one of the struggling readers raised his hand and wanted to share his book, one of *The Magic School Bus* books. [The other students] were so supportive, and the higher readers even made connections to their own books, which opened up time for some of the other low readers to participate with their books. I just let the conversation go on for about 10 minutes. It was such an incredible experience for me to be a part of."

Jason didn't initially identify building community as an important part of his vision. However, as a former employee at a behavioral hospital, Jason had firsthand experience with the effects of isolation and loneliness. Jason's actions in his classroom showed that he was adding the importance of community building to his vision for teaching, even as he was navigating what role community building would have in his instruction.

their topics so that they can find the materials and information they need to develop and complete their projects.

Ask your students these questions to guide them:

- What do you want to learn more about? Why?
- What materials do you think you need, and where can you find these materials?

See Appendix A for other texts to support developing students' agency.

CHAPTER 2

What Is Purposeful Teaching with Literature?

WHAT'S THE BIG IDEA?

Purposeful teaching builds on knowledge and beliefs about teaching. It requires that teachers possess a vision, consider students' identities and interests, and adapt the curriculum to support students. In this chapter, we focus on teaching visions and how they contribute to the teaching of children's literature and to structuring purposeful reading opportunities in classrooms.

WHAT ARE THE THEORIES?

Visioning

A vision is "a teacher's conscious sense of self, of one's work, and of one's mission . . . a personal stance on teaching that arises from deep within the inner teacher" (Duffy, 2002, p. 334). A vision offers inspiration to teachers about how they wish to structure their classroom and about the skills they want to develop in their students and in their work as professional educators. Beliefs are based on past experiences, whereas visions look to the future. Teachers who possess a vision have a direction and a long-term plan for their instruction and possess what Duffy (2002) calls "an independent spirit" (p. 333). These visions guide teachers in their instructional decisions, influence student learning (Darling-Hammond & Bransford, 2005), and are based on past experiences and teachers' knowledge. For example, the vision of Ms. Thomas, a fifth-grade teacher, was shaped by her own educational background. As a student of color who struggled to read, she was very focused on developing her students' agency for social justice. She wanted them to make choices about what they wanted to read and how they wanted to share. As a result, she began implementing "Genius hour" (Smith, 2017) in her classroom. See Chapter 7. She began by setting aside 45 minutes every other week for students to choose a topic of their choice, conduct research, and share with the class. She acknowledged that this practice was not something that the administration supported, but her response is, "This is something my students need!" Consider these vision statements from other teachers with whom we've worked:

- Mr. Jee, a seventh-grade teacher: "My vision is to create thoughtful, independent, inquisitive young people who can collaborate with one another and have a sense of leadership and who can lead."
- Ms. Klay, a fifth-grade teacher: "I want to create independent readers who are motivated and who want to read on their own."
- Ms. Owin, a third-grade teacher: "I want them to have a love for learning. And that one of the ways that they learn is through reading, getting information through writing out their ideas, and sharing their ideas with other people. It's to have that love for learning, because that is going to carry them through into their adult life, no matter what it is they choose to do. If they don't have that, then their opportunities are shutting down in front of them."

These thoughtful visions connect what these teachers believe about their students with their own knowledge and their purpose for teaching. These examples of teachers' visions are enacted in practice through a variety of instructional choices.

- Mr. Jee structures book clubs where students self-select their texts and hold student-led discussions of texts.
- Ms. Klay invites her students to interview one another and find common issues to research. She asks students to work with one another to pursue a topic of interest, find resources at the school library, and work together to display information to the class on their topic.
- Ms. Owin invites her students to create their own learning targets for reading. She asks them to reflect on something they want to improve through reading and invites them to work with her to create a plan to do so.

Visions serve as guides for teachers as they strive to implement instructional practices reflective of their ideals. Enacting a vision for reading can occur in all aspects of instruction. Consider a guided reading group in another classroom. Ms. Kim, a first-grade teacher, introduces making connections to students. The students are given Post-it Notes to track their thinking as they read the guided reading book independently. A few minutes into the reading time, the teacher stops the students and says:

"We're going to work on making connections. What about this story makes sense to you and why? Let's think about the events and things that have happened in your life. Can you make a connection with the main character in the story?"

When asked to explain this action, Ms. Kim explained:

"I want them to see that reading is something you can do to make sense of the story but also of what's going on in their lives. Reading can help my kids. They can use these stories to figure out all kinds of things that are going on in their lives."

Much like Ms. Kim and the other teachers we've discussed, the teacher becomes the balancing factor for the reader (see Figure 2.1). This means that the teacher is using his or her vision, beliefs, and knowledge to establish a balance of texts and tasks that will help keep the student engaged, as well as introduce the student to new ideas and knowledge.

As this figure shows, the reader is at the center. These instructional practices are connected to these teachers' visions for students as readers. Ms. Kim and Ms. Thomas want their students to become inquiring learners who can use reading as a tool to make sense of their lives and experiences. Visions can shape teachers' actions in the classroom and serve as a thoughtful plan for teachers to envision and develop their ideal classroom. These visions demonstrate "a strength and

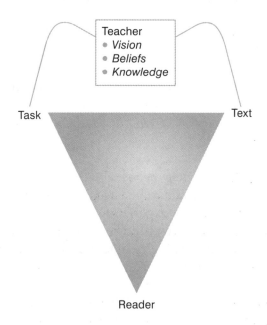

FIGURE 2.1. Adding the teacher relationship.

professional dignity that suggest[s] that these teachers go beyond pedagogical competence. They possess a sense of mission that allows them to maintain an independent stance in the face of the pressures to conform and comply" (Duffy, 2002, p. 339).

Visions must be anchored to instructional practices tied with one's beliefs and one's knowledge of students and teaching that can help sustain teachers when the demands of teaching become overwhelming. Gambrell, Malloy, and Mazzoni (2011), emphasize that "without a vision the teacher is left to sway and sputter as a candle facing the winds of curricular change and federal, district, and school-level impositions" (p. 21).

Visions must change and shift over time. Consider another teacher with whom we work. Ms. Nelly, a second-grade teacher, believes that students should have choices and decision-making power with respect to reading literature. When asked about her vision, she shared, "I want my students to be able to make decisions and get excited about reading and to see what reading can do for them." However, her vision was in conflict with the types of instructional practices she adopted. She used the prescribed literacy curriculum program, which offered a limited choice in texts for students. As she reflected on her vision, she began to make small changes in her classroom. First, she introduced a short 20-minute window of literature circle time in her class to give her students a choice of texts and time for discussion. But after seeing how engaged and excited her students were with reading texts of their choice, she put the prescribed literacy curriculum aside and incorporated literature circles during her main reading instruction time. When asked again about her vision, she shared the following:

> "I want my students to have their own agency when it comes to reading. Agency means having choices about what to do and how to do it. Student agency is about choice and can range from a lot to a little of freedom of choice; it can apply to what is being learned as well as how it is learned. The bigger role students have in deciding what they want and how to do it, the more student agency there is. When I decided about what they had to read, they really had no agency."

Visions bring together teachers' beliefs about their teaching practices, their students, and their experiences, and can be used as tools to help structure learning opportunities. As Ms. Nelly's experience shows, visions and the types of instructional practices aligned with our visions are not fixed but change as our knowledge and beliefs about teaching change. As we become more knowledgeable about what works and what doesn't, we should alter and make revisions to our visions.

Teachers develop visions about children's literature and cultivate a vision of themselves as teachers of children's literature, a vision of their students as readers, and a vision of their classroom as a literate environment where students feel comfortable about reading. But how do you connect a vision inclusive of developing and supporting agentic readers that is aligned with instructional practices? We believe that teachers must adopt a purposeful approach to teaching that places the reader at the center. In the following section, we discuss a purposeful teaching approach in more detail.

PRACTICAL CONSIDERATIONS: WHAT DOES A PURPOSEFUL APPROACH TO TEACHING LOOK LIKE?

Purposeful teaching incorporates knowledge about pedagogy, the students we teach, and visioning. In the context of using children's literature in reading, we recommend the TACKLE approach (Time, Access, Consider, Keep, Listen, and Engage) to align your teaching within a purposeful frame. This purposeful approach to teaching builds on what research tells us about effective reading instruction related to tasks, texts, and readers.

Time

Students need targeted time to read. This concept is called reading volume (Allington, 2012). Reading volume is defined as the combination of time students spend reading and the number of words they actually read (Allington, 2012) and supports vocabulary development, knowledge of subject matter, and diverse perspectives. Research emphasizes that students who read more in terms of sheer minutes and numbers of books have higher achievement scores than students who read less (Allington, 2012). This relationship is demonstrated repeatedly in diverse fields. Those who achieve expert status as musicians and athletes share at least one thing in common and it's not natural aptitude. Rather, it is the time they spend in purposeful practice (Ericcson, Prietula, & Cokely, 2007). Just as an athlete will not achieve the desired results by watching others play or practice, students will become better readers by spending more time engaged in reading. Remember, as noted in Chapter 1, that Gambrell (2015) found that in a recent survey of reading habits of children ages 6–17, only 33% of students surveyed reported that their class had a specific time during the day devoted to reading a book of their choice. Students are more encouraged to read when they have a choice about what they read. Unfortunately, without the element of choice, students may be less likely to want to read. When students don't read, the chances of them developing the habits of a lifelong reader drops, as well as their projected achievement in reading.

Sadly, from our observations across dozens of classrooms, we rarely see kids reading. For example, consider a recent conversation we had with a student:

MARGARET: What did you do at school today?

STUDENT: We worked on doing math facts fast.

MARGARET: What kinds of things did you do for reading?

STUDENT: We didn't really do reading.

As this conversation indicates, we know all too well that reading has taken a back seat during literacy instruction. As teacher educators who are passionate about reading, we are upset when students share that they don't want to read because reading at school is boring. We know about the lack of reading time in schools and the alarming frequency of instructional time spent reading and extracting information from photocopied stories or reading shortened stories from core programs.

In fact, within the last 18 years in classrooms we've visited, the amount of time we've documented students spending time reading is meager. Typically, in the classrooms we've observed with experienced teachers, their lessons are filled with extensive teacher talk, teacher modeling, worksheet completion, and teacher read-alouds. Such experiences during literacy instruction coincide with national educational trends that have restricted teacher autonomy and adaptability during literacy instruction. With the passage of the NCLB in 2001, classroom teachers across the nation had to teach reading using prescriptive literacy programs that provided teacher scripts outlining extensive teacher talk and minimal time for student choice in reading. Although the NCLB has been replaced, its lingering effects remain as we continue to see a lack of reading time in many classrooms. Devoting time every day to giving students a choice of books of interest to read is critical.

Access

Access to high-interest, authentic, and culturally responsive texts is essential. Authentic literature reflects the worlds that students experience daily in their lives in and out of school (Gambrell, 2015). Two examples highlight the mismatch between the desire to offer students access to authentic texts and the constraints of school budgets.

First, schools spend significant parts of their budgets on core literacy programs that promise to provide all the necessary reading materials. We know of districts that spend between 5 and 10 million dollars, respectively, to adopt new core literacy programs. The reading materials provided with these programs are limited and are offered within a scope and sequence framework that gives teachers and students very limited choices of texts or topics.

Doesn't the school library offer authentic texts that students and teachers can choose? The answer to this question is not as positive as one might hope. In a recent conversation with a school librarian who shared the observation that across many districts, librarians simply aren't given a budget for new books. If librarians want new books, they are asked to seek funding and raise money for them through external grants. She continued, "What usually happens is that we spend most of our money on items like tape to repair the books that we have." Second, the system for using the school library is not always conducive to engaging students with texts. Unfortunately, not every school has a school librarian. In schools that still do, the school librarian is the technology teacher/paraprofessional/lunch-and-recess-duty monitor and has minimal time to share his or her knowledge of literature with students. Frequently students who have access to a school library may have less than 10 minutes to check out a book. Even worse, many students are limited to checking out books within their level and/or are required to read, and take tests on, a specific number of books based on the district's leveled computer reading program, practices that researchers have found to be counterproductive to students' reading achievement and intrinsic motivation to read (Thompson, Madhuri, & Taylor, 2008).

Given the limited access to quality texts, the need for effective teachers—and their classroom libraries—have become essential. Consider Sarah. Her role as an effective reading teacher depends on knowing books and knowing them well. Over time, she has created a classroom library with books grouped by genre, rather than by level. She encouraged her students to read texts that interested them, regardless of level. There are many stories of educators like Sarah, who go against the grain to promote reading during literacy instruction. We work with many of these teachers on a daily basis, but we continue to wonder: Why is it that reading and providing opportunities for students to read interesting, engaging texts and materials go against the grain today during literacy instruction? Time and access to high-interest books of choice are essential when providing a purposeful approach to literacy instruction.

Consider

Consider a flexible approach to teaching reading and one that values students' diverse cultural, historical, and linguistic backgrounds.

Choose purposeful literature, texts, and materials that are culturally relevant to today's increasingly diverse and rich student population. Scholars highlight the role of a culturally responsive understanding (Au & Mason, 1983; Gay, 2010; Ladson-Billings, 2005) in which texts and materials align with students' traditions, backgrounds, and stories. Considering diverse texts in your classroom library is paramount.

Keep

Keep the main thing about reading instruction—actual reading. Teaching explicit skills during reading instruction is important, but it is equally important to provide opportunities for students to read texts of their choice so they can develop the habits of a reader and a love of reading. Many approaches to reading instruction allow for student choice. Decades of research outlines multiple perspectives on reading engagement that consists of developing motivational dispositions in students, cognitive strategies, and conceptual understanding in reading, and fostering discourse and discussion using authentic literature. Encourage skilled teachers who have a vision for teaching reading that fosters a love of reading in students and permits them to make decisions about the texts and materials they read and share with others. Cochran-Smith and Lytle (2009) emphasize the role teachers can have in leading professional development and educational change through careful thought and reflection.

Listen

Listen to your students. Find out what students want to read and then let them read it. Choice is a powerful motivator. The reverse is also true. Asking students to read books that they are not interested in decreases motivation to read (Ivey & Fisher, 2006). Often, giving students choice means letting them read books that might not make it on the list of "teacher-approved" literature, or books that we think are appropriate for kids. We've heard more than one teacher say they hate the *Diary of a Wimpy Kid* (Kinney, 2007) books, and librarians say graphic novels aren't real books. Listen to students about what they value and want to read.

To make room for books that kids choose, we need to get rid of ephemera leftovers from literacy programs, such as copies of tired basal programs and stories. Since we both taught *Mrs. Wishy Washy* (Cowley, 1993) nearly 15 years ago, there has been considerable progress in increasing the availability of high-interest, culturally relevant texts for students. Encourage students to engage with authentic and inviting texts based on their interests. Taking the advice of the popular tidying guru Marie Kondo (2014), we suggest inviting students to ask, "Does this spark joy?" If it doesn't, thank it for its service and get rid of it in your reading baskets and classroom libraries.

Provide opportunities for students to read authentic literature. Doing so doesn't mean that every single book used in the classroom is one that students choose. Introducing students to new books and intriguing information is essential in developing knowledge of the world. Opportunities for students to share their opinions and make decisions about the kinds of texts they would like to read is imperative in fostering and developing lifelong readers (Ivey & Johnston, 2015; Wilhelm & Smith, 2014).

Engage

Let students engage with books and with each other. By *engage*, we refer to helping students develop relationships with the characters and authors in the books and with one another around books. Classroom-based research has repeatedly documented a strong social component of letting students choose what books to read, followed by opportunities to talk with other students (Ivey & Johnston, 2015; Wilhelm & Smith, 2014). Over time, students are able to talk with one another about how they relate to the characters in books; this, in turn, can influence their relationships with one another. Further, as readers engage with each other, they begin to form identities as readers. Reading is no longer viewed as the domain of "smart people" but as a practice accessible to all. A strong reading identity can support a writing identity. The fan fiction genre emerged from a sense of wanting to participate with the characters of a text. Online access makes it relatively simple to write to an author. Blogs and other online platforms support students' understandings that reading and writing can be about relationships between authors, readers, and characters that blur the lines of distinctions between authors and readers.

No child has ever been excited about reading a condensed story in a completed worksheet or about a story that's been read to them for 5 consecutive days. Keeping the TACKLE approach in mind can allow for students' agency in reading.

PRACTICE

The theories we've just outlined help to explain why it is important to have a belief system, a vision, and an understanding of a purposeful teaching approach to using children's literature in your classroom. They also suggest a view of how reading can serve as an authentic and meaningful outlet for students. To summarize:

1. Reading for an authentic purpose is essential.
2. To enjoy reading, students need opportunities to read at school.
3. Students must have choice in what they read.
4. Developing reading volume in students is an important dimension of reading instruction.

In this practice session, you are invited to reflect on becoming purposeful in your approach to reading and using children's literature. You will be asked a series of questions about becoming a reader and your own experiences with reading. Then, you will reflect on and write about your reading vision and detail the instructional practices that support a purposeful approach to reading and using children's literature. In this session, you are also invited to read a case example of a practicing teacher's vision aimed at supporting empowered students.

ACTIVITY 1. *Reflecting on the Reading*

1. Reflect on how you can structure your classroom to set aside time for students to read authentic and engaging literature. Notice the books that are worn

out. Are there particular series that students seem drawn to? Create a list of popular texts in your classroom and work to expand the number of books of the same genre or by the same author. Ask your colleagues what the popular books are in their classrooms. Most important, ask students what are their favorite books, and why?

2. How can you provide more access to texts and more opportunities where you consider students' voices, interests, and perspectives during reading times? Think strategically. Ask yourself the following questions:

   a. What books represent the specific students with whom I work? Are these books reflective of their lives and experiences?

   b. When I visit with students, what are they interested in? How can I find resources about the topics and interests they have?

   c. How can I have student check-ins about their preferences? Consider organizing a schedule in which you interview your students about their changing perspectives and interests about texts. You can ask them to share what are they currently reading and what are their favorites and why. If students stumble with answering these questions, dig deeper and ask them more about their interests.

Seek the help of your school librarian, other students, and colleagues for additional recommendations.

ACTIVITY 2. *What Is Your Vision?*

1. What is your vision for reading and for children's literature in your classroom? Write a vision statement about what you envision for your students concerning reading in your classroom. The following are possible areas to think about and select from as needed when writing your vision statement.

   a. *Time:* How much time do you want to allot for reading?

   b. *Access:* How do you provide a variety of texts for students to read?

   c. *Consider:* What does a flexible approach look like to you when incorporating children's literature?

   d. *Keep:* How will you provide time in your class for students to read more, and to read texts of their choice?

   e. *Listen:* What do your students think about the books they read? How can you create a check-in system for you to know what students think about the books they read?

   f. *Engage:* What are some ways you can have students engage with books? Revisit your vision bimonthly and reflect on what you wrote. Has anything changed? What are you doing to support aspects of your vision? Are you experiencing any barriers? If so, what supports can you elicit to help you navigate these obstacles?

2. Give your students the following reading inventory. What topics, books, and ideas interest them?

   Reading Inventory
   a. How do you choose a book?
   b. What kinds of books do you like to read? Why?
   c. What are the topics you are interested in learning more about?
   d. What was a positive experience you've had when reading? Why was it positive?

ACTIVITY 3. *Case Study*

Read the case study in Box 2.1 of Tonya, a first-grade teacher of 9 years. Reflect on the questions about her vision and how it shaped her instruction.

1. Describe Tonya's vision in the following areas: teaching, learning, students, and literacy.
2. How did Tonya's beliefs influence her instruction?
3. Midyear Tonya had a schoolwide directive to adhere to the prescriptive literacy program outlining a skill and drill approach to reading instruction. This included prescribed texts for students, worksheets to demonstrate targeted skills, and a one-size-fits-all approach to reading instruction. What might have been the areas of conflict for Tonya between outside expectations and her own beliefs? How might she respond to these conflicts?

ACTIVITY 4. *Using Children's Literature: Extra Yarn*

Consider how texts can be used to learn about students' visions in reading. Using read-alouds, model to students how to cultivate their own vision about reading. Ask them about their vision as learners and readers. What do they want to work on as learners and readers? What types of reading materials do they want to read and why? A powerful text that can be used to model this to students is *Extra Yarn* (Barnett & Klassen, 2012). In this story, a young girl named Annabelle knits clothing for everyone in her community. Her vision is to knit and create something beautiful. Although she faces obstacles, she persists and learns how to fulfill her vision in the story.

See Appendix B for additional texts to use when talking about visioning with students.

BOX 2.1. A Portrait of Visioning in a Classroom

Tonya's vision centered on wanting to develop empowered students who acquired skills and made consistent progress in reading as they engaged in meaningful literacy activities.

Tonya shared the following about her vision: "By empowered, I want my students to feel confident about their reading abilities and to view reading as something they could do."

BUT WHAT DOES THAT LOOK LIKE IN PRACTICE?

To accomplish her vision, Tonya designed her classroom to include a variety of activities such as literature circles, interviewing partners about books they created during Writer's Workshop, and independent reading time during which students could read anything in the classroom. She created an extra activity in her class called Read Anything in which students were encouraged to roam the room and find anything of interest to read. By creating these multiple opportunities for her students, she hoped that they would improve upon their existing strengths and skills as readers and writers and be able to navigate classroom activities meaningfully. Students were encouraged to talk about books with one another. Tonya reasoned that her students needed a variety of opportunities to learn targeted skills, to do independent reading, and to collaborate with peers.

She also structured real-world meaningful activities to encourage her students to become a part of the community around them. For example, during one year of teaching, the NASA robot explorer, Phoenix, was scheduled to land on Mars, and her students were excited about the topic of space. Tonya launched a unit on space and used online resources to engage the class. Students worked with each other to learn more about space. One group met with the librarian, and another group interviewed experts about space. Then, working in pairs, students chose how to display the information they learned through videos, podcasts about space, and posters.

CHAPTER 3

What Matters When Teaching with Literature in the Classroom?

WHAT'S THE BIG IDEA?

In the previous chapters, we looked at the role that beliefs and vision play in purposeful teaching. In this chapter, we focus on the content knowledge needed when using literature. Purposeful teachers use beliefs, vision, and content knowledge as a checks-and-balances system. Beliefs and vision without content knowledge about teaching and literacy will fall short; content knowledge without beliefs and vision will also fall short when trying to teach in a purposeful manner.

This chapter considers the task, the text, and the areas of content knowledge, as illustrated in Figure 3.1. The type of task that students are asked to use can be linked to three broad literary theories: New Criticism, reader-response, and critical theories. The texts that students are asked to read are commonly divided into genres. As the image shows, the most important component in the relationship between tasks and texts is the reader. Only a knowledgeable and visionary teacher can provide the balance and integration required to meet the needs of the reader.

WHAT ARE THE THEORIES?

Theories help us focus on and clarify our own beliefs regarding the roles of the reader, the text, the tasks, and the contexts (Snow, 2002). It is our position that teachers must be purposeful about how they approach the text and the theories

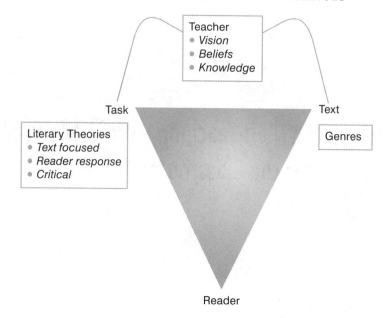

FIGURE 3.1. The teacher–reader–text–task relationship.

they teach with the text. Serafini (2009) wrote, "The ways in which children's literature is used in the elementary classroom are directly related to the teacher's definition of reading, her beliefs about how meaning and knowledge are constructed, and the role of the reader in the act of reading" (p. 17).

In this chapter, we discuss three types of theories that influence the teaching of literature: New Criticism, reader response, and critical theories.

1. New Criticism theories posit that there is a correct meaning of the text that can be discovered through a close study of the text (Applebee, 1994; Hinchman & Moore, 2013).

2. Reader-response theories posit that the meaning does not reside in the text, but in a transaction with the reader (Rosenblatt, 1978, 1994).

3. Critical theories examine texts with a consideration of the constraints and the supports of cultural, political, and historical systems (Serafini, 2009). These critical theories include culturally responsive pedagogies (Gay, 2010; Ladson-Billings & Tate, 2006; Nieto, 2000; Vasquez, 2014), and are especially important as they have caused the field to adopt a more inclusive approach to children's literature (Garcia & O'Donnell-Allen, 2015; Gay, 2010; Paris & Alim, 2017).

Literary theories offer differing perspectives on how reading is defined, how meaning and knowledge are created, and the roles of the teacher and reader. Which theory is the "right" theory? We can hear the frustration now: "I just want to know how to be a better teacher; theories are for college professors." That's what we used to think, but over time we have realized that we were enacting theories every day simply by using the activities that we chose and by how we structured our classroom. For example, asking students to read a text and then underline the author's argument and evidence is based on a theory. In this case, it is the New Criticism theory, according to which meaning is found in the text alone and that the purpose of the teacher is to help students become better and better at correctly understanding what a text means. In another example, in teaching mini-lessons focused on making connections, we are using the reader-response theory, as we ask readers to transact with the text to make their own meaning and a connection to what they read. Theories are important to know because they guide our decisions as teachers and ultimately what we ask of our students. Theories are based on beliefs about texts, readers, and teaching and ultimately determine what activities are used to teach with children's literature.

Literary theories are also reflected in every curriculum series and professional development opportunity. Recognizing that theories are foundational elements of curricula and training helps us evaluate the curricula we are asked to teach and the information we are receiving. Serafini (2009) articulated this beautifully:

> Teachers are often forced to adopt reading programs that tell them how to teach, regardless of their beliefs and understandings. Classroom teachers need to understand contemporary theories of reading and literacy development and be able to articulate their theoretical perspectives concerning children's literature, the reading process, and their instructional practices, so they do not fall victim to the political pressures associated with standardized tests, state-mandated curricula, and commercial reading programs. (p. 17)

In short, theories may focus on the role of the text, the author, the reader, or context-oriented approaches. Our intent is not to provide an exhaustive review of literary theories. Instead, we focus on three of the most common theories that influence the curricula and approaches used in elementary and middle schools. We describe each theory, followed by a section that considers the practical constraints and affordances of the theory.

Text-Focused Literary Theories

In text-focused theories, the roles and influences of context, author, and reader are purposefully excluded from consideration. The focus is on the text exclusively and its message. In other words, the message needs to be extracted from the text by the reader. A popular text-focused theory is New Criticism, in which the reader uses textual analysis through close reading to analyze and arrive at the meaning in the text.

The text-oriented theoretical approach is clearly demonstrated in the CCSS. For example:

> The Common Core State Standards place a high priority on the close, sustained reading of complex text, beginning with Reading Standards 1. Such reading focuses on what lies within the four corners of the text. (Revised Publishers' Criteria; NGA & CCSSO, 2012, p. 4)

> Text-dependent questions do not require information or evidence from outside the text or texts; they establish what follows and what does not follow from the text itself. . . . When examining a complex text in depth, tasks should require careful scrutiny of the text and specific references to evidence from the text itself to support responses. (Revised Publishers' Criteria; NGA & CCSSO, 2012, p. 6)

Text-focused theories help readers stay close to the text. There is no room for personal stories about parallel connections to the text. There are correct responses to what the text is about and incorrect responses to what the text is about. Materials that support this method of text interpretation emphasize literal information (the main idea, conflict, resolution, etc.), procedures for close reading, and methods for annotating text. These procedures and methods can be applied to almost any text. Assessment typically includes standardized tests or measurements that show the correctness of interpretations about a text.

Close reading is intended to help students identify and understand what the text says, initially without focusing on a personal response to the text. According to Shanahan (2017), this initial figuring out is meant to come from reading, rereading, and discussing, instead of from teacher-led instruction. Shanahan goes on to pose a three-pronged framework for close reading, which we have revised for clarity:

- First read: The purpose is comprehension, and answers the question "What is the text about?"
- Second read: The purpose is figuring out how the text works, and answers the question "What components did the author use?"
- Third read: The purpose is to evaluate the text, the author's point of view, and answers the question "What does this text mean?"

Reader-Response Theories

In contrast to textual theories in which meaning resides in the text, reader-response theories view meaning as something that resides in the reader or in the transaction between the reader and the text. Instead of deriving a single meaning from a text, multiple meanings of texts can exist based on the reader's point of view and the experiences each individual brings to the text. Interpretations are not without some limits in that they should relate to the text, but the main directive of this theory is that the reader connects and responds to the text. Just as individuals are different, so too are readers' responses and connections to texts. This theory supports these differences and invites readers to make their own meaning and connections to the text.

One of the most well-known reader-response theorists is Rosenblatt (1988), who described reading as a transaction:

> Every reading act is an event, a transaction involving a particular reader and a particular configuration of marks on a page, and occurring at a particular time in a particular context. Certain organismic states, certain ranges of feeling, certain verbal or symbolic linkages, are stirred up in the linguistic reservoir. From these activated areas, to phrase it most simply, selective attention—conditioned by multiple personal and social factors entering into the situation—picks out elements that synthesize or blend into what constitutes "meaning." The "meaning" does not reside ready-made in the text or in the reader, but happens during the transaction between reader and text. (p. 4)

Reader-response theories privilege readers in the sense that multiple interpretations of a text are acceptable. The challenge for teachers rests in evaluating the interpretations. Does accepting multiple interpretations mean that any response is acceptable? What should happen when students' background experience and interpretation are clearly holding them back from understanding what's in the text?

We often observe this when students read expository texts and are faced with new information that challenges their previous understandings about a topic. For example, consider a read-aloud about germs with kindergartners in Mr. Keon's class. Before reading the text *Those Mean, Nasty, Downright Disgusting but Invisible Germs* (Rice, 1989), students made a chart that listed what they already knew about germs. They wrote, "All germs are bad," and "Every time you get a germ, you get a fever." After a read-aloud of this text, along with other books about germs, students added what they learned to the chart as a result of what they had just read. In this way, through literature, students are able to revise their understandings and make new connections to extend their thinking and learning.

Students' prior knowledge is a double-edged sword that can aid comprehension but can also interfere with it (Block & Pressley, 2002). We talk more about the role of background knowledge when reading texts in Chapter 7, but this example demonstrates how children's literature can serve as a means for students to challenge their thinking and add to what they know (and don't know).

Helping readers gain knowledge is not a simple or fast process. Reader-response theorists suggest that encouraging students to read widely and to talk with each other about what they read are important steps in helping them understand that there are multiple points of view and interpretations about texts. In this way, according to reader-response theories, making sense of the text resides in the reader, in the interaction between the reader and the text, and between readers through discussion of the text. A reader-response approach allows for the possibility of multiple interpretations.

Structures to support discussions look different depending on the specific students with whom you work, the instructional objective, and the overall goal for students. In some cases, the teacher enters the discussion as a knowledgeable participant who purposefully guides discussion and reading in order to open up children's interpretations of the text. Taking the student back to what a single text says, not unlike what the text-oriented theories suggest, may be appropriate to guide students into deeper comprehension.

There are two general approaches to soliciting connections from students. In one approach, the teacher models specific kinds of connections, generally summarized as text-to-self, text-to-text, and text-to-world. Using the book *Crown: Ode to a Fresh Cut* (Barnes, 2017), a teacher could tell students that the first part of the text reminds her of a time when she went with her father to get a haircut. She might then explain that another phrase we use when a book reminds us of something from our lives is a text-to-self connection. Then students could be asked to share their own text-to-self connections. If making connections is new to students, the teacher might model or focus connections to text-to-self connections.

A different approach to teaching students about making connections is to read a text aloud and pause only to ask, "Does anyone have something that this reminds them of?" These connections are written down. After the students have read the book, the connections are sorted, much as words are sorted, and they are asked to suggest their own names or labels for groups of connections. One third-grade classroom came up with their specific list of connections, including differentiating between connecting to a book and connecting to a movie or other visual source. In one type of connection, they realized that they needed to make their own visual images, while in the other connection, they recognized that they were relying on someone else's visual idea.

Critical to either approach of helping students make connections is helping them to evaluate connections. Some connections help the reader make sense of text, whereas other connections distract from this purpose. For example, when thinking about the book *Crown*, one connection might be a time when I took a pet to the groomer. When I revisited this connection, I realized it was a distracting one that did not help me understand the characters or text in any way. It is important to allow students the opportunity to explain if a connection helps them or not, rather than try to evaluate them at first. Some connections may not be apparent to the teacher but can still help the student. The teacher's role is simply to continue to ask students to think about and explain how the connections help them understand the text in a deeper way.

Context-Oriented Theories

The third group of theories is collectively referred to as context-oriented theories. These include feminist literary theory, gender theory, and Marxist theory. In these various theories, texts are considered to be the products of a larger context, such as genre, politics, gender, or nationality, as well as viewed in the context of which groups have power and which ones do not (Klarer, 2004; Serafini, 1993). Klarer (2004) gives the following example:

> In Marxism, texts are analyzed as expressions of economic, sociological, and political factors. Conditions of production in certain literary periods and their influence on the literary texts of the time are examined. A Marxist literary interpretation, for example, might see the development of the novel in the eighteenth century as a consequence both of new economic conditions for writers and readers and of new modes in the material production of printed books. (p. 94)

Context-oriented theories regard meaning as something created from social practice. Meaning is negotiated as part of a social interpretation, either with others or with the contexts and/or authors. Texts must be questioned for influences from the larger context, as described by Serafini (1993):

> A critical perspective on reading assumes that there is no neutral, context-free construction of meaning. Reading is a social practice that cannot be separated from its political and cultural context. A critical perspective focuses on the larger social, political, cultural, and historical contexts in which reading and other literate activities are practiced. . . . Rather, literature is used as a vehicle to provide a space for critical conversations, discussions that go beyond the walls of the classroom to include the political, cultural, and historical contexts of the world in which we live. (n.p.)

In classroom practice, readers are taught to ask questions about the larger context and to understand how they are positioned by various contexts (Serafini, 1993). With this theory, students and teachers may struggle to dig deeper into critical conversations (Kelley, Stair, & Price, 2013), leaving them with unresolved ideas and understandings about genre, politics, gender, or nationality, as well as about who has power and who does not.

WHAT'S THE RIGHT THEORY?

In our efforts to be better teachers, we may find ourselves asking which of these theories is the best one. The answer is . . . all of them. Each theory can be stretched to an extreme, lessening its use for practical instruction in the classroom. For example, an extreme focus on textual theories could result in students being asked to conduct close readings of almost every text they encounter, accompanied by detailed annotations and searches for what the text really means. If students only engage in this kind of reading, they are likely to be unmotivated to read and hesitant to offer answers for fear they will be incorrect. They may miss the joy of connecting with a text and being able to describe how the text makes them feel.

Alternatively, reader-response theories taken to extremes can result in students spinning rambling quasi-connections to text that do not support comprehension, and in teachers who are hesitant to consider any response as incorrect. Context-oriented theories can also result in such a narrow focus on one particular contextual influence that other ideas are excluded or even devalued. In each case, it is not that the theory is inherently wrong. Instead, it is the application of the theory that goes astray. Thus, we argue for an adaptive and purposeful approach.

We encourage you to carefully consider what theories are represented through particular activities and then aim for a balanced application of a theory. You might not be able to achieve this balance with a single text. When reading a historical novel, initial activities might be rooted in reader-response theories, so that students can think about how the characters feel, and whether they have ever had similar feelings. For example, when reading *One Crazy Summer* (Williams-Garcia, 2011), you might ask questions such as, "Is your relationship with your brother, sister, or friend similar or different from Delphine, Vonetta, and Fern's relationship?" In later chapters, you might ask, "Why did the sister's mother think the Black Panther's work was important?"

PRACTICAL CONSIDERATIONS

How Do You Plan for Using Children's Literature?

Once you conceptualize which theories align with your vision and beliefs, it is helpful to approach the wide range of books available when you teach according to a classification system. Genre is a classification of texts into types or categories. A range of text types for grades kindergarten through eight emphasizes three broad categories of genres: poetry, narrative, and informational text. Within each of these broader categories are smaller categories. For example, a narrative might be a folktale or a realistic fiction text. A poetry text might be free verse or haiku verse.

Key Distinctions

Narrative genres typically have a distinct structure, in which the characters interact, try to work on a problem, and find a resolution. Although we often think of narratives as fictional stories, narratives also include nonfiction accounts, such as memoirs, autobiographies, and travel writing.

In thinking about narrative texts, we often mistakenly assume that because a narrative belongs to this broad category it is always fiction. However, there are narrative expository texts that have typical key features that deviate from narrative fiction. Think about the two subcategories in this way.

Expository genres typically are arranged in one of the following text structures: cause and effect, problem–solution, descriptive, or chronological. More than one text structure is commonly found within longer texts, such as a text that contains a chronological structure within a broader descriptive pattern. Text features such as bolded text, photographs, captions, charts, graphs, infographics, maps, and headers are common in expository genres. (See Chapter 7 for more on expository texts.)

These categories, or genres, help describe what readers might expect to find within the text (see Table 3.1), and help them think about the purpose for reading when they begin a text. For example, in an expository genre, one expects to find nonfiction texts that describe something true about the world or about a person. In narrative texts, one expects to find a story arc that develops around the pattern of characters, settings, problems, and a resolution or resolutions.

Additionally, because students connect with information delivered in different ways, it can be useful to integrate multiple genres into a broader topic of study. For example, *They Called Us Enemy* (Takei, 2019) is an autobiography told through a graphic-novel genre and offers a broad view of one family's experience. *Barbed Wire Baseball* (Moss, 2013) tells the true story of Kenichi Zenimura, a Japanese American baseball player, who went on to play baseball with players such as Babe Ruth, as a picture book. *Paper Wishes* (Sepahban, 2016) is the fictionalized account, told in first person, of a young girl and her family's experience with being forced to move to an internment camp. These titles can be enhanced with other texts, such as maps, infographics, and newspaper accounts. Providing a range of genres invites students to access information in different ways, to connect with the characters in different ways, and to consider why authors make the choices they do when they tell stories.

We periodically check the websites of the following organizations for their updated book lists organized by genre:

- National Council of Teachers of English
- American Library Association
- Young Adult Services Library Association
- International Literacy Association
- United States Board on Books for Young People (Outstanding International Books List)

See Appendix C for specific book titles within these genres.

TABLE 3.I. Genres and Their Characteristics

Genre	Characteristics
Folk literature (folktale/fairytale)	*Setting:* Imaginary worlds, often vague (long, long ago). Magic is common to folk literature.
	Characters: Typically portrayed as good or evil. There are often witches, wizards, talking animals, or characters that use magic. Many characters conform to a stereotype, such as a wicked stepmother or a faithful friend.
	Problems: The characters often face seemingly insurmountable odds and thus, need the help of friends and/or magic.
	Events often occur in sets of three.
	Resolution is often a version of happily ever after, while emphasizing themes such as compassion, generosity, and humility.
Science fiction	*Setting:* Imaginary worlds, often futuristic or historic.
	Characters: Often portrayed as good or evil.
	Problems: The characters often face scientific or technological advances and major social or environmental changes, frequently portraying space or time travel and life on other planets.
Realistic fiction	*Setting:* Real or imagined modern-day places.
	Characters: The characters are meant to be familiar, as if they are people that the reader might meet.
	Problems: The characters face problems that target audiences will be familiar with, such as family upheaval, school challenges, and relationship complications.
Historical fiction	*Setting:* Frequently a real place in the past. If the place is not real, the description will offer something so realistic that it may seem real to the reader.
	Characters: The characters are often a mix of real historic characters and imaginary characters.
	Problems: Authors explore both problems of the period depicted, such as typhoid fever, as well as modern problems that have challenged people throughout time.
Poetry	Poetry can be in a variety of forms, including haiku, couplets, cinquain, and concrete. Each form is governed by its own set of traditions. Free verse poetry may read more like a narrative and tell a connected story.
Narrative nonfiction	Narrative nonfiction is a specific type of nonfiction wherein true events are presented in a narrative style using literary techniques. Biographies, autobiographies, and memoirs are often written in this style.
Expository nonfiction (problem–solution, cause–effect, chronological, sequential)	Expository text is typically arranged in a descriptive, chronological, cause–effect, or problem–solution structure. However, many expository texts are a blend of text structures, such as a book that describes a scientific theory in a chronological way.
Graphic novels	Graphic novels may be any of the above genres. The defining feature of graphic novels is the use of panels or pictures. The pictures are critical to the overall understanding; without the pictures, some of the story might be incomprehensible.

Blended Genres

Although many texts fit within the above categories, others are considered blended categories, which means that they have the characteristics of more than one genre. For example, Jerry Pallotta's popular *Who Would Win* series combines both expository and narrative formats. In the first two-thirds of the book, the facts about animals are presented in traditional expository formats with many charts, graphs, and infographics. In the final third of the book, a fictional battle is imagined between two animals, such as a polar bear and a grizzly bear (in other books in the series, battles are based on an event that could happen). A more common blending is the way free verse poetry is used to tell a narrative story, such as in Kwame Alexander's (2014) *The Crossover* or Jacqueline Woodson's (2014) *Brown Girl Dreaming*. In these cases, the narrative features of character, setting, conflict, resolution, and themes are evident.

White Bird (Palacio, 2019), a graphic novel, is a wonderful example of a book that blends many genres and features. It begins with Julian, a character from Palacio's (2012) book *Wonder*. There is a brief reference to the events from *Wonder*, before the story shifts to an exchange between Julian and his grandmother, told through panels that suggest a FaceTime conversation using both French and English words. The book then turns to a story of the Holocaust, blending real facts with a made-up story line. At the conclusion of the book, the author's notes offer explanations about what part of the story is true and how she conducted her research. *White Bird* is an example of a blended format. The book does not fit into a single category but instead uses multiple genres to communicate something that the author is passionate about.

In the classroom, this book can provide a rich experience that guides students in a discussion of genre. A first step can be simply showing the panels on a document camera to introduce the story. Next create a chart showing which events are real and which events are fictional. Then, ask students to (a) consider why the author told the story in this way, and (b) how the story would have been different if it were told in another way, such as through prose rather than a graphic novel format. If there is time, allow students the opportunity to write about a single event in two separate genres or through one blended approach.

PRACTICE

Understanding the role of theories and genres is essential when using children's literature to structure purposeful reading opportunities in the classroom. The New Criticism, reader-response, and critical theories are foundational in the sense that they can help to situate the types of texts and tasks and the roles of the reader when structuring reading opportunities. Noticing how a genre approach can support structuring authentic opportunities is particularly helpful when planning for them.

ACTIVITY 1. *Reflection Questions*

1. Consider the reading tasks you've encountered in your school career, from elementary school through college. Were the tasks you were given based on the New Criticism, reader-response, or critical theories? What were the benefits and challenges of these tasks?

2. As a reader, which genres of texts do you read most often? Least often? How might your own reading habits affect your students' reading preferences?

ACTIVITY 2. *Evaluating the Theories behind Your Literacy Program*

Choose a single lesson from your curriculum or from one readily available online. Analyze the tasks presented by categorizing them as questions from text-focused theories, reader-response theories, or context theories. If activities don't seem to fit into one of these three categories, create at least one miscellaneous category and create a title that describes the activities. For example, some activities might deal specifically with practice questions for test preparation. They might be labeled "test-taking practices." Looking through the lesson, what area (text-focused theories, reader-response theories, context theories, or other theories) is most represented? What area is least represented?

Choose a second lesson, preferably one that uses a different text genre, and categorize the activities within the lesson. Do the activities from the second lesson follow the same pattern, or do they represent a different theoretical background?

Reflect on your findings. As a teacher, or as a teaching team, is there a theory that is omitted in your lesson evaluation that should be included? What might those lesson activities look like? How do the additional activities support your stated beliefs?

ACTIVITY 3. *Case Study*

Consider the following directions from a fourth-grade teacher's guide. Students are asked to read a historical fiction selection about the American colonists' desire for freedom from the British. The teacher is directed to deepen pupils' understanding of the story's theme by contrasting the freedom of choice given to the main characters. Students are asked to discuss questions such as the following:

- Do you think "The Second Lantern" is an appropriate title for this story? Why?

- What did Mr. Wentworth mean when he said, "You've lighted a lamp for freedom?"

- What does the word *patriot* mean in this story?
- Would Jon have called himself a patriot at the beginning of the story?

This activity is from the 1965 teacher's guide *Ventures* published by Scott Foresman (Robinson et al., 1965). An example of a more contemporary curricula is a fourth-grade lesson from the EngageNY (New York State Education Department (n.d.) modules, which offer questions that are not unlike the 1965 lesson.

> Say: "We are going to read section two a third time. Let's look at some of the language used here. Who is 'she'? Why do the Haudenosaunee refer to the Earth as 'Mother'?" Have students share their thoughts with a partner and write their notes in the margin. Call on some students for their ideas. Focus on the sentence "Now our minds are one." Ask students to think about what that sentence means.

Both of these lessons are based on a text-based theory. Students are asked to find meaning within the text. They are to define the word *patriot* based on how it is used in the story. They are asked to analyze language usage and read a passage multiple times. Neither of these lessons asks students for a personal response or for a response that relies on prior experiences.

ACTIVITY 4. *Using Children's Literature:* **Wishtree,** *Applying* **Reader-Response Theory**

Consider how texts can be used to invite students into the learning and into reflecting on their own experiences and learning about how to connect with others.

Wishtree (Applegate, 2017) is a powerful story about Samar, a young Muslim immigrant who recently moves to a community where there is an old red oak. People write their wishes and hang them on the tree. However, one boy posts a hateful message on the tree about Samar and her family. The story discusses what is done to combat this example of hatred in the community.

Using this text, ask students to make a connection to the characters in the story. Have there been times when they felt isolated and alone? Ask students to explore the strengths of the main character who faces discrimination in her community. Connect the text to the world around us, and invite students to think critically about injustices in their local community, state, nation, and the world, and the actions that can be taken to work against them.

CHAPTER 4

What Do Books Have to Offer?

WHAT'S THE BIG IDEA?

As we noted earlier in Chapter 1, our population is growing increasingly diverse, in terms of racial, ethnic, socioeconomic, and religious diversity, and more. *What do books have to offer given these social trends?* The broad answer is that books offer an opportunity for students and teachers to see themselves and others in what they read, to learn about others who are different from them, and to learn to function within a community that values each other's voices and learns from one another in a respectful way.

WHAT ARE THE THEORIES?

Literature is a powerful tool and can help children see themselves, others, and the world beyond their front door. It has an essential role in developing a world-view that is inclusive; that harnesses the funds of knowledge students possess; and that provides a window, mirror, and a sliding glass door for students (Bishop, 2009), emphasizing the use of multicultural texts to provide those opportunities.

Funds of Knowledge

Students come to class with rich stories, languages, experiences, beliefs, and knowledge. Understanding and valuing students' lived experiences outside of school are essential components of seeing what students have to offer each day. To do so, we need to think of students as having funds of knowledge (Moll,

Amanti, Neff, & Gonzalez, 1992), wherein their cultures and experiences are honored and viewed as assets. Such a perspective is in stark contrast to a deficit-oriented perspective that views students as lacking abilities, knowledge, and experiences. Instead, harnessing students' funds of knowledge allows for inviting their diverse cultures into the mainstream classroom and views students from an asset-based perspective that prompts teachers to ask, what resources can I use to honor and support my students and how can I incorporate their knowledge and strengths to help them succeed?

Understanding this funds of knowledge viewpoint is particularly essential when thinking about and teaching with children's literature. Teachers can elicit funds of knowledge and build on their students' cultural resources when using children's literature. In this view, children have agency and are not passive participants. Instead, children bring their own stories, ideas, languages, and experiences that are essential to incorporate into the classroom. Bishop (1992) states, "if literature is a mirror that reflects human life, then all children who are or are read to need to see themselves reflected as part of humanity" (p. 43).

Children's literature can be used to invite students' cultures, languages, and experiences into the classroom. For example, teachers can incorporate texts that are culturally relevant and meaningful to students. To illustrate, Shelly, a Native American teacher with whom we work, invites students' stories and cultural ways of knowing into the classroom. She reads aloud *Trickster: Native American Tales* (Dembicki, 2010) with her fifth graders and invites them to create their own graphic novels using coyotes, rabbits, and crows. When asked why she includes culturally responsive texts in her classroom, she shared, "They can't find books because there are no books . . . I want to validate them and who they are" (Vaughn, 2016, p. 37). In this way, teachers can use texts and materials that reflect the specific students with whom they work, thereby supporting and honoring their linguistic and cultural backgrounds.

Windows, Mirrors, and Doors

Readers' imaginations use books to allow them to live different lives (Huck, 1997; Johnson, Koss, & Martinez, 2018) and to experience situations that are new and unfamiliar. When texts act as mirrors, the readers see some aspect of themselves reflected in them. When readers cannot find themselves reflected in the books they read, or when the images they see are distorted, negative, or stereotypical, they learn a powerful lesson about how they are devalued by the society of which they are a part (Bishop, 1990):

> Books are sometimes windows, offering views of worlds that may be real or imagined, familiar or strange. These windows are also sliding glass doors, and readers have only to walk through in imagination to become part of whatever world has been created or recreated by the author. When lighting conditions

are just right, however, a window can also be a mirror. Literature transforms human experience and reflects it back to us, and in that reflection, we can see our own lives and experiences as part of the larger human experience. Reading, then, becomes a means of self-affirmation, and readers often seek their mirrors in books. (p. 9)

Johnson and colleagues (2018) extended the sliding glass door metaphor by describing it as a conduit for change:

> Books that serve as sliding glass doors are somewhat akin to a window experience but with a key difference: The reader is changed by the book. Often, this occurs when a reader meets characters who are changed by their experiences. Books that serve as windows allow readers to look and to visit. Books that serve as sliding glass doors invite readers to step through and into an experience that may change them. The change may not be visible to others and may not be immediate to the reader. Sometimes, though, the reader, like the character, is motivated to take action in ways that will transform his or her world. (Freire, 1970, p. 572)

If literature is to serve as windows, mirrors, and sliding glass doors, teachers need to be purposeful about including books that reflect students in various ways, while also giving them access to books that offer a variety of perspectives. This body of literature is expanding, providing more books that represent children's diverse backgrounds and ethnicities. In 2017, the percentage of books published by or about people of color and native people hit 31%, an all-time high. Although this number is not as high as it should be, this is a step in the right direction. Books that represent the social and cultural experiences of underrepresented groups are termed multicultural literature, and include those that focus on race, ethnicity, sexual orientation, gender, disability, and language.

There are multiple benefits of using multicultural literature in your classroom.

- Students feel pride in their identities and cultural groups when they read literature that highlights their culture and the experiences of languages, cultures, and groups they represent.
- Students learn that society is complex and diverse, in which many important and varied perspectives are represented instead of a singular perspective.
- Students develop a balanced historical perspective reflective of the struggles, obstacles, and triumphs experienced by people and movements in U.S. history.
- Students can read literature to explore complex issues of social justice (Au, 1993, 2015).

Reading as an Invitation to Share

Just as books offer windows, mirrors, and doors, they can also offer invitations for students to value and share their own stories. Oral storytelling and writing are important ways for students to begin to share their voices.

Oral Storytelling

Stories are told every day across communities. People share stories as a way of passing on ideas to others. Stories tell us about the common characteristics of a culture and can be used to pass on these ideas to subsequent generations (Kovach, 2010). The oral storytelling practices of many cultures is a powerful tool with which to communicate stories across generations. For example, the oral traditions of people of African descent serve as a way to preserve the rich stories and experiences related to traditional values and rituals.

Native American stories using various natural elements such as the sun, the mountains, and the sea, as well as animals like the coyote, are important elements in stories told by elders, family members, and entire communities to pass on and share lessons with others. Storytelling empowers people by "unshrouding the lives of those who have come before them . . . and enabling people to have a clear picture of their situation and the options available to them" (Banks-Wallace, 2002, p. 412). Central to purposeful teaching is supporting the act of oral storytelling in the classroom and inviting family and community members to share their stories with students and teachers.

Writing

Writing is an important way for students to begin to share their voices. Researchers and practitioners frequently agree that reading widely is an important part of becoming a writer (Gallagher & Kittle, 2018). Smith (2006) stated:

> All the nuts and bolts of writing—including spelling, punctuation, and grammar, but more importantly the subtle style and structure of written discourse, the appropriate organization of sentences and paragraphs, and the appropriate selection of words and tones of voice—are learned through reading. The point deserves emphasis. *You learn to read by reading and you learn to write by reading.* (p. 188)

One of the perhaps unintentional outcomes of the CCSS, and the successive curricular materials, is a narrowing of what students write about. The CCSS Anchor standards (e.g., CCSS.ELA-Literacy W.4.1) for writing ask students to write arguments, informative/explanatory accounts, and narratives. Many publishers and teachers interpret these standards very narrowly, so that students in kindergarten are writing only opinion pieces and personal narratives. The written products usually reflect an academic style emphasizing the use of traditional syntax, grammar, and paragraph form—in direct contrast to the most popular children's books, such as *Diary of a Wimpy Kid* (Kinney, 2007), the *Plants vs. Zombies* series (Tobin, n.d.), and other books that use comics, line drawings, and other images to communicate.

In *Write Like This*, Gallagher (2011) stated, "If we are to build students who grow up to write in the real world, we must move our writing instruction beyond a 'cover the state standards' mind-set by introducing our young writers to additional real-world discourses" (p. 8). Such real-world discourses are modeled through a variety of written texts that are not limited only to books. But those discourses are only accessible to students if they are encouraged to read widely and are supported by being encouraged to write in a variety of genres and modalities.

The key to supporting students who read (and write) broadly is choice. Certainly, students need to be asked to read and write within genres they might not otherwise try. At the same time, researchers repeatedly confirm that students want choices about what to read and what to write (Allington & McGill-Franzen, 2018; Zumbrunn et al., 2019). In thinking about the types of texts you select in your classroom, keep in mind that students need opportunities to choose texts they are interested in. One way to provide choice while structuring your classroom library to represent multiple perspectives is to select texts that are inclusive of well-written multicultural and award-winning books.

For many years, the most referenced children's book awards were the Caldecott and Newbery awards. The Caldecott Medal was named in honor of the 19th-century English illustrator Randolph Caldecott. It is awarded annually by the Association for Library Service to Children, a division of the American Library Association, to the artist who creates the most distinguished American picture book for children. Books on the final runner-up list for the Caldecott award are designated as Honor books. The oldest children's book award in the world is the Newbery Award. Its criteria, as well as its long history, continue to make it the best-known and most-discussed children's book award in this country. Books receiving the Newbery Award are honored for the interpretation of the theme or concept; presentation of information, including accuracy, clarity, and organization; development of plot; delineation of characters; delineation of setting; appropriateness of style for literary quality; and quality of presentation for children. Honor books are also designated for the final runner-up list.

In addition, we have a wealth of awards that value many kinds of cultures and diversity. For example, the Pura Belpré Award, established in 1996, is presented annually to a Latinx writer and illustrator whose work best portrays, affirms, and celebrates the Latinx cultural experience in an outstanding work of literature for children and youth. And the American Indian Youth Literature

Award was established in 2006 and honors exemplary writing and illustrations about Native Americans and Indigenous peoples of North America. According to the American Indian Literature Association (AILA), books that are selected to receive the award "present Indigenous North American peoples in the fullness of their humanity" (AILA, n.d.). See Appendix D for lists of awarded children's books organized by award name

PRACTICAL CONSIDERATIONS

How Do You Build a Classroom Library That Is Inclusive of Diverse Perspectives?

Students can only experience windows, mirrors, and doors if they have access to a wide range of books. Relying on the school library to meet this need is often insufficient since there are many weeks when the library is unavailable and students are usually limited in the number of books they can check out. Allington (2012) suggested that a single classroom needs about 1,500 books in order to provide the breadth of topics to capture students' interests, multiple books about the same topic to sustain their interest, and books at multiple levels to accommodate a variety of readers. Although collecting such a large number of books might seem impossible, there are steps you can take to improve your collection.

Here are some points to keep in mind when planning your library:

- Include a variety of books from across multiple perspectives.
- Use the checklist shown in Figure 4.1 to review books to ensure they are culturally responsive.
- Create text sets that are culturally responsive and organized by geographic region and theme (see Figure 4.2 on p. 48).
- Look at the book-award selections to help you locate texts that are culturally relevant (see Appendix D).
- Consider how you will display the books. Students are more likely to choose books whose covers are visible, so think about using baskets and trays and rotating what students see.
- Rotate some books in and out of your library to keep students interested.
- Collect multiple copies of the same text so that students can read together.
- Consider how you will keep track of books in your classroom library. A checkout system can be very helpful.
- Don't be afraid to cull books at the end of the year, letting students take home books that look well loved. Most students won't pick up a book that looks worn unless they already have a connection to the book.
- Keep adding recently published books to your collection, reflecting specifically on the diversity that they add to your library.

How Do You Find Authentic Multicultural Literature?

Authentic multicultural literature allows for multiple voices and perspectives to enter your classroom. Although the number of multicultural books from which to choose is growing, how do you find well-written multicultural books that are authentic and devoid of racial and cultural stereotyping? Cultural details such as dialect, customs, and clothing must be represented accurately.

The Anti-Defamation League (n.d.) has created an extensive list of resources to help educators create equitable classrooms. We have adapted their guidelines into a Checklist for Choosing Multicultural Books (see Figure 4.1).

Sonia, a fifth-grade teacher (referenced in Chapter 1), was outraged by the text *Voyage of the Half Moon* (West, 1995), recommended as part of the required state curricula. The text disparaged Native American students as "these people" and "devils" (West, 1995, pp. 2–3). Using the Checklist for Choosing Multicultural Books, we can examine *Voyage of the Half Moon* and ask the following questions:

- Is the text written by someone of this culture and/or someone who has extensive knowledge of the specific culture?
- Does the story offer themes that reflect the narrative in a realistic and non-judgmental manner?
- How would a child of that ethnicity or culture feel after reading the text?
- Are the characters devoid of racial and/or cultural stereotyping?
- Do "good" characters represent a variety of backgrounds?

After answering these questions, you'll be able to determine that the *Voyage of the Half Moon* is not a text that meets the necessary criteria for being a quality multicultural text, illustrating the importance of carefully examining texts to ensure cultural authenticity.

Where Do We Find the Money to Build a Classroom Library?

Finding the money to create an extensive classroom library is challenging. Like most teachers, we spend a lot of our own money on books. Although small grants can help create libraries, the books you acquire will belong to the school if you decide to leave. We found that we didn't want to part with our books. We haunt used book stores, library sales, and warehouse sales, and put books on our wish lists. To create our list of books, we consider sources such as #weneeddiversebooks, award lists, best-seller lists, and of course our students. We ask them about books they like and why. We talk to librarians and ask them what books we should be adding to our collection.

One way we have added to our libraries when we didn't have money to spend is to ask our students to author books. The book can be as simple as a picture with a caption in the lower grades or a wordless comic in the older grades.

Story	Are the stories interesting to children?	
	Are there story elements for children to explore (e.g., conflicts, themes, plot)?	
	Are conflicts resolved in a manner that is nonstereotypical?	
Characters	Do the characters represent a variety of nondominant ethnic or cultural groups?	
	Do "good" characters represent a variety of backgrounds?	
	Are characters devoid of racial and/or cultural stereotyping?	
Themes	Are values being explored and not preached?	
	Does the story offer themes that reflect the narrative in a realistic and nonjudgmental manner?	
	Are cultural settings represented realistically?	
Illustrations	Is there diversity represented within cultural groups?	
	Are characters represented in a realistic manner?	
	Do illustrations avoid reinforcing societal stereotypes?	
Voice	Is the story written by someone of that culture and/or someone who has extensive knowledge of the specific culture?	
Other considerations	Are children exposed to multiple perspectives?	
	Are the stories age appropriate?	
	How would a child of a nondominant ethnicity/culture feel after reading the text?	
	Do the stories promote an understanding of our diverse society?	

FIGURE 4.1. Checklist for choosing multicultural books. Questions adapted from the Anti-Defamation League (n.d.).

Multiple students might contribute to a genre study on infographics or a theme study on inventions. Individual student-authored pages can be laminated and bound to create physical copies, or scans can be formatted into a PDF document and shared on a class-share site. We find that student-authored books serve to elevate interest in topics and books, while validating students' authentic writing opportunities.

Another low-cost way to build your classroom library is to develop text sets. Text sets are collections of texts that focus on a single overarching concept. By using text sets, we can avoid the problem of having enough copies of the same books for everyone. These multilevel collections about the same topic allow students to become increasingly independent, permitting them to begin to make choices about which texts they'll read and how they'll demonstrate an understanding of them. They provide opportunities for creating social interaction as students become "experts" about a text and share their knowledge with their classmates. Text sets offer exposure to multiple genres and a variety of perspectives on a topic.

In creating a text set, we consider how to include texts that vary in three ways. First, we consider texts that have a range of reading levels. Second, we consider texts that include a range of subtopics or time periods within the overarching topic we are considering. Third, we consider how to represent multiple genres and/or text formats within the text set by mixing fiction, nonfiction, poetry, graphic novels, and materials in addition to books by including websites,

---

Afghanistan Text Set

Nasreen's Secret School: A True Story from Afghanistan (Winter, 2009)

Listen to the Wind (Mortenson, 2009)

Four Feet, Two Sandals (Williams & Mohammed, 2007)

The Kite Runner (Hosseini, 2011)

The Sky of Afghanistan (Eulate, 2012)

Parvana's Journey (Ellis, 2015)

Oppression and Inequality Text Set

Dolores Huerta: A Hero to Migrant Workers (Warren, 2012)

Martin's Big Words (Rappaport, 2007)

Separate Is Never Equal: Sylvia Mendez and Her Family's Fight over Desegregation (Tonatiuh, 2014)

Gleam and Glow (Bunting, 2005)

Lost and Found Cat: The True Story of Kunkush's Incredible Journey (Kuntz & Shrodes, 2017)

A Song for Cambodia (Lord, 2015)

FIGURE 4.2. Two sample text sets.

audio and visual media, and infographics. Figure 4.2 shows examples of two text sets: an Afghanistan text set and an oppression and inequality text set.

Books offer an opportunity for students to see themselves and others and to learn about other sociocultural experiences. By giving them access to a wide assortment of books about a wide range of characters and topics, students access information about others. They also access their own voices so that they can communicate their stories with others.

PRACTICE

Using texts to support and engage students is paramount. Understanding the role of students' out-of-school lives, lived experiences, and home languages is essential when structuring purposeful reading opportunities. By using a variety of awarded children's literature, as well as specific ways to analyze texts, you can ensure that the texts you introduce to students are inclusive of diverse perspectives.

ACTIVITY 1. *Questions for Reflection*

1. What might the mirrors, windows, and sliding glass doors metaphor mean to your students? How might it help to develop students' agency?

2. Can you reflect on a powerful multicultural book that you've recently read? Review the book according to the criteria outlined in Figure 4.1. How do you find a well-written multicultural book?

ACTIVITY 2. *Planning List for Your Classroom Library*

1. What would your ideal classroom library look like?

2. Think about the books in your ideal classroom. How will you select books for your classroom to align with your reading vision?

3. Do you have books representative of a variety of cultures, identities, languages, and socioeconomic levels? Are students seeing books reflective of their cultures and identities and those of others? Are your books suitable for discussion? Do you have high-interest and engaging series books?

ACTIVITY 3. *Case Study*

Read the case study in Box 4.1 of Sonia, a fifth-grade teacher of 12 years. Reflect on the questions about the ways she used multicultural literature and how it shaped her instruction.

BOX 4.1. A Portrait of Multicultural Literature in the Classroom

Sonia is a Native American teacher who teaches at a school with a high percentage of Native American students. Sonia's vision centered on wanting to develop knowledgeable students who were empowered and acquired a love of reading. She emphasized that she wanted her students to be able to see themselves in the books she read. She shared the following thoughts about her vision:

> "Way back when grandmas would tell the kids about stories, Coyote was always the one they used to tell the stories, but the books that they put in the curriculum don't have stories about Coyote or books about us. It's important for us to do this [develop this curriculum], not only for them to become better readers and writers, but just with Native students, that they have a way to express themselves. And so it's something that we really have to work on, for them to be able to say that's me, I'm here and to be able to communicate what they're thinking, and how they feel."

To meet this need, Sonia developed a unit on the lifecycle of the butterfly with Coyote. Coyote represents many things, such as a guide, courage, and teacher. Students created their own texts in their Native language and in English where they asked Coyote questions about butterflies, the local landscape, and activities, and Coyote answered them with facts that the students researched and wrote about. To supplement this unit, Sonia incorporated a variety of texts in which students could see themselves, such as *Trickster: Native American Tales, a Graphic Collection* (Dembicki, 2010), and *Thirteen Moons on Turtle's Back: A Native American Year of Moons* (Bruchac & London, 1992). In addition, she invited tribal elders, and family and community members to visit her classroom and share their stories about the local community and community activities that were important to her students. In so doing, Sonia worked to embrace the third space (Moje et al., 2004), a space in which "there is an integration of knowledge and discourses drawn from different spaces . . . merging the 'first space' of people's home, community, and peer networks with the 'second space' they encounter in more formalized institutions such as work, school, or church" (Moje et al., 2004, p. 41). Sonia further shared, "I want them [students] to each hear a different story. It wouldn't just be just one perspective or two perspectives, but them actually just talking to an Elder and hearing stories and having them be heard" (Vaughn, 2016, p. 37).

1. List the actions Sonia took to adapt her instruction to support the use of multicultural texts.

2. How did Sonia's knowledge about teaching, about her students, and about texts influence her instruction?

3. When adopted curricular programs texts include texts that are not culturally responsive, what can you as the teacher do?

ACTIVITY 4. *Using Children's Literature: How to Create a Text Set on the Theme of Justice*

In this activity, we invite you to create your own text set on the theme of justice. We've provided three possible books to use in this text set. Try to add at least five additional texts that would illustrate the theme of justice.

Text Set on Justice
- *Malala's Magic Pencil* (Yousafzai, 2017)
- *Brave Girl: Clara and the Shirtwaist Makers' Strike of 1909* (Markel, 2013)
- *The Youngest Marcher: The Story of Audrey Faye Hendricks, a Young Civil Rights Activist* (Levinson, 2017)

As you add to this text set, try to create a range of levels, assuring that multiple readers have access to the content even if some students cannot read every text in the text set. Additionally, aim for a range of topics. For example, in a theme about justice, we don't want every book to be about the Civil Rights movement of the 1960s. Instead, as the three books already in our text set show, we consider justice at different periods of time and for different groups of people. Finally, the text set can represent multiple genres and formats. Not every book needs to be nonfiction. Students may be able to empathize with fictional characters in a way that they do not with historical figures. Further, not everything in the text set needs to be a book. Consider adding artwork, infographics, audio and visual media, websites, and other types of content.

CHAPTER 5

How Can We Help Students Understand the Books They Read?

WHAT'S THE BIG IDEA?

There is no silver bullet as far as using children's literature in the classroom. Moreover, as much as we love books, we can't simply put lots of books in our classrooms and expect all students to read with understanding. There are no set instructional practices that are guaranteed to support comprehension. At the same time, we can describe several components of supporting comprehension that effective teachers use as they weave their knowledge of practice, of students, and of books in order to help students understand the books they read.

WHAT ARE THE THEORIES?

In this section, we discuss reading comprehension, represented at the top of Figure 5.1, as a theory and goal for instruction. In the classroom, comprehension is supported in many ways. We highlight three areas that support comprehension and that are also shown in the figure: adaptive teaching, gradual release of responsibility, and translanguaging.

Comprehension

Comprehension as a theory is relatively new to education. For much of the past 2 centuries of schooling, teachers of young children were more concerned about students being able to memorize and recite works rather than being able to explain what they were about. During several decades in the 20th century, learning to read was based on the look–say method, in which students read texts that

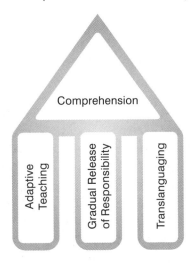

FIGURE 5.1. Supporting comprehension.

introduced new words within a controlled ratio; for example, beginner texts read, "See Spot run. Run, Spot, run." Any meaning to be made came from looking at the pictures. These books were not inclusive but rather depicted white, middle-class children with no attention to diverse cultures, languages, and experiences.

It was not until the late 1970s that comprehension came to be considered a critical component of elementary education. It was thought that if students learned comprehension in their early school years, they would not need extended instruction on the process in the upper grades. By the 1980s, researchers were focusing on how readers thought about a text. The reader's cognitive processes were documented through think-aloud protocols. Pressley and Afflerbach (1995) catalogued over 90 reading strategies used by readers. They developed an extensive list of the many comprehension-monitoring strategies employed by readers, which they grouped into three large categories: identifying and learning text content, evaluating text, and monitoring understanding.

One of the original authors returned to this idea 15 years later. Afflerbach and Cho (2009) wondered what, if anything, readers did differently when reading through websites. They found that readers still used these same three large categories for understanding text but identified a fourth group of strategies that readers used to support comprehension: realizing and constructing potential texts to read. That is, when readers go to the Internet to search for a particular topic, they essentially create their own text when they choose a search result and then follow a variety of links, back arrows, and new links.

Despite the numerous strategies readers used to understand a text, Pearson and Cervetti (2017) observed that a reader's comprehension is still puzzling:

> Comprehension, or understanding, by its very nature, is a phenomenon that can only be observed indirectly. People tell us that they understood, or were

puzzled by, or enjoyed, or were upset by a text. Or, more commonly, we quiz them on the text in some way. All of these tasks, however challenging or engaging they might be, are little more than the residue of the comprehension process itself. (p. 13)

The question then is how should comprehension be taught using children's literature? Beginning in the 1980s and continuing in many curricula today, instruction has focused on the cognitive elements of comprehension. This cognitive focus emphasizes teaching students ways to think when approaching texts, such as monitoring their comprehension, using fix-up strategies, and summarizing. Commonly, teachers introduced a strategy, such as predicting or questioning. They modeled the strategy with a read-aloud. Students were invited to try the strategy and document their thinking. While this approach makes for a nice, neat instructional method, the reality is that most readers do not use just one strategy at a time while they are reading. For example, a reader can make connections, ask questions, and infer what might happen next in a text. Further, one reader may use one strategy to understand a text, and another reader may use a different strategy to understand the text. Finally, the scope and sequence of teaching in this manner became muddled. If the readers "learned" an inferring strategy in third grade, did they need to repeat it again in fourth grade? What should be taught if students already know the comprehension strategies?

In the past two decades, educators have emphasized moving beyond a focus on cognitive strategies and thinking of ways in which comprehension is achieved through students' interactions with their own past, their present experiences, and their future goals. This view is sometimes referred to as the sociocultural view. Specific to comprehension, this view holds that readers are sense makers (Aukerman, 2008). Multiple readers make multiple meanings of a text. Further, a student can be actively making meaning and arrive at a conclusion that might not agree with the teacher or curriculum's conceptions. The teacher's job is to facilitate this meaning making and seek to understand how the child is making meaning with the text, rather than simply look for particular interpretations of the text. Instruction that aligns with this view of comprehension would include multiple opportunities for students to interact with and discuss their understanding of texts and ample time to talk about texts with peers. Cognitive strategies would be introduced with the idea that they were an invitation to help students make sense of the text and that they might not practice the strategy in the same way that it was modeled. To support reading comprehension, teachers must be adaptive and flexible in how they teach with children's literature. We explore adaptive teaching as a means of supporting students' individual learning needs.

Adaptive Teaching

We ground our literacy practices within the broader instructional theory of adaptive teaching, which documents that teaching is flexible and can accommodate the complex linguistic, socioemotional, and instructional needs of students. Given the increasingly diverse student population in the United States (Kena et al., 2015) and increased attention to standards, adaptability is an essential tool required "to [fit] the demands of teaching more complex versions of literacy" (Kamil, 2016, p. 239).

The concept of adaptability has a long history in the field of education. Formative educational theorist, John Dewey (1933), suggested the need for an adaptive approach to teaching:

> Flexibility, ability to take advantage of unexpected incidents and questions, depends upon the teacher's coming to the subject with freshness and fullness of interest and knowledge. There are questions that he should ask before the recitation commences. What do the minds of pupils bring to the topic from their previous experience and study? How can I help them make connections? What need, even if unrecognized by them, will furnish a leverage by which to move their minds in the desired direction? What uses and applications will clarify the subject and fix it in their minds? How can the topic be individualized; that is, how shall it be treated so that each one will have something distinctive to contribute while the subject is also adapted to the special deficiencies and particular tastes of each one? (pp. 276–277)

More recently, Duke, Cervetti, and Wise (2018) found that exemplary literacy teachers modified grouping structures; changed instructional goals and objectives depending on what instructional skills students needed next; and developed instruction specific to the individual instructional, cultural, and learning needs of their students. Adaptive teachers reflect on their practice, know their students well, and have a vision (Vaughn, Parsons, Gallagher, & Branen, 2016).

Gradual Release of Responsibility

Gradual release of responsibility (GRR) describes a framework in which responsibility for doing a task is transferred from the teacher to the student. Without attending to this transfer, it is easy for instruction to remain very teacher driven. The roots of such scaffolded instruction originate in Vygotskian theory, particularly associated with the *zone of proximal development* (ZPD), in which a more expert learner provides the appropriate support, or scaffold, to a novice in order to help the student achieve a goal that the learner cannot yet master independently (Vygotsky, 1978).

There are typically four components of this type of instruction: a focus lesson in which explicit instruction might be provided, followed by guided instruction, collaborative practice, and independent practice. On the surface, GRR appears to be a straightforward, sequential process. In fact, this is the way that it has been practiced in much literacy instruction. For example, the teacher might read aloud a segment of the text and think aloud about how she asks questions of the text. Next she asks students to listen or read with her, and they make connections together. Then students practice with another segment of the text and work collaboratively to make connections, before being asked to make connections independently.

However, this application of the theory is an oversimplification of what a scaffold is intended to do. The interaction between an expert, or teacher, and learner is complex, requiring expert knowledge, judgment, and decision making. For example, the teacher must determine when to provide support and when to release control to learners. Moreover, the teacher assesses the knowledge of the learner throughout the scaffolding process, skillfully modeling, demonstrating, and introducing tasks that are just within the ZPD, while incrementally advancing to the ultimate goal. At the same time, the teacher appropriately releases control to the learner, while assessing the learner's progress in assuming greater responsibility toward reaching the goal. As with explicit teaching, GRR must be used in an adaptive way rather than as a predetermined sequence of steps.

Translanguaging

Many of our learners are multilingual. They use whatever language knowledge they have to make sense of the text. Translanguaging is the use of two (or more) languages in order to more fully comprehend a text and communicate that understanding to others (García & Wei, 2014). This practice draws from an assets-based pedagogy that leverages and values students' cultures, languages, and heritage. The use of multiple languages to discuss one common text supports students' heritage language, their overall retention of information, and their ability to connect to known information.

In a particular translanguaging literacy practice called TRANSLATE (Teaching Reading And New Strategic Language Approaches To English learners; Goodwin & Jimenez, 2015), a teacher reads aloud a section of text with her Spanish-speaking bilingual students. Students focus first on obtaining an overall meaning, using Spanish, English, or a mix of the languages to retell. Next, the teacher (and over time, the students) selects one or two key sentences to translate from English into Spanish. Students then discuss and evaluate their translations.

We view translanguaging as one of the multiple components of adaptive teaching. In this case, emphasizing and valuing the utility of all languages and heritages creates a space for all learners to appreciate language and learning. At the same time, a pedagogical approach, such as TRANSLATE, offers specific instructional goals that are similar to explicit teaching and GRR since students are given particular ways of approaching the text.

The theories we've outlined help to explain why it is essential to have an understanding of adaptive teaching in your classroom and the need for a vision inclusive of a flexible approach to using children's literature. They also suggest a view of how to connect your reading vision to these ideas. The big ideas discussed include:

1. Teachers are adaptive when using texts in the classroom.
2. Teachers use their knowledge of explicit teaching, gradual release of responsibility, and translanguaging to model, support, and encourage independence with texts.

No single program can meet the needs of all of your students. It's the teacher's responsibility to build on students' funds of knowledge (Chapter 4) and to connect his or her knowledge of practice, of students, and of books in a balanced way. It takes knowledge of all of these dimensions to be adaptive. The goal of these instructional practices is that of supporting reading comprehension. These three approaches to using children's literature are critical to supporting reading comprehension. By understanding when and how to use and adapt instruction, GRR, and translanguaging, a teacher is better able to develop instruction to meet student needs.

PRACTICAL CONSIDERATIONS

How Do You Engage Students Meaningfully with Texts?

Purposeful teaching that is adaptive can be daunting. You might be asking, "How can I ever do all of that?" Let us offer two practical suggestions: know your students and know books. In the following sections, we discuss these two suggestions.

Teaching Comprehension Requires Knowledge of Students

Adaptive teachers know their students well. Specifically, teachers need to know about students' backgrounds and experiences in order to create meaningful learning opportunities for them (Banks et al., 2005). They need to know about their students' home cultures, their language development, and their interests.

There are a variety of ways to get to know your students, including interest inventories, individual conferences, and observations. We recommend all of them. As you get to know your students better, take the time to build community with the whole class. Practices such as read-alouds and "bless this book" (Marinak & Gambrell, 2016) support more learning about and from books (see Box 5.1 and Chapter 6 for more on this topic). They also help to create a shared point of reference among the class. For example, one teacher jokes "I need another gelato" when things aren't going very smoothly. The class typically laughs and they try again. The rest of the teachers and students in the school don't recognize the short quote from *Olivia Goes to Venice* (Falconer, 2010), which creates a feeling of belonging for the class.

Another resource for fostering community within a class is to adopt some of the warm-ups used in the theater. These community-building activities

BOX 5.1. Ms. Netson: Using "Bless This Book" to Support Student Choice

In Ms. Netson's second-grade class, students lead their own "bless this book" to support opportunities for student choice and agency in the classroom. Each day, one student gets to lead the "bless this book" talk. Students get to decide how they want to share the books—in small groups, with a peer, or with the teacher. Ms. Netson knows that giving them a variety of choices in texts is essential. She is aware of her students' interests. She has a high percentage of Latinx students in her classroom who are full of rich language knowledge and experiences. To support her students, she selects a variety of texts they can choose from that represent strong portraits of girls and boys from diverse nondominant backgrounds and cultures as well as books based on students' interests. See the Appendices D and E for examples of texts that resonate with students' linguistic and cultural backgrounds.

have gained popularity well beyond the theater, including their use by leadership teams in major corporations. For example, creating silent charades allows students to use their bodies while silently negotiating with partners or small groups. Theater warm-ups and team building focus on using the whole body, using space, and interacting with others.

Teaching Comprehension Requires Knowledge of Books

There is no specific way to improve upon your knowledge of books. Talk to people. Make friends with librarians. Follow blogs and TED talks. Learn the stories behind the books. For example, Brian Selznick told an interviewer (Grant, 2011) that much of the plot for *Wonderstruck* was inspired by his desire to draw lightning. Jacqueline Woodson (Woodson, n.d.) works on multiple books at the same time because she gets bored with one plot. Grace Lin (2016) shared that the books she now writes, focused on Asian American children, are the kinds of books she wished she had available to her when she was a child.

More than all of these things—read. Read lots! As you do, we recommend starting by reading books within two broad groups—what adults select for kids to read and what kids select for themselves and other kids to read.

What Adults Select for Kids

We recommend reviewing the most recent book lists from the Association for Library Service to Children. The lists include bilingual books for children that have not won awards because the selection of these books so far is small. Additionally, the National Council of Teachers (NCTE) hosts a blog called Build Your

Stack, which lists a variety of books focused on a single topic, such as "affirming the diversity of Black hair." The lists are composed by children's book authors, teachers, and other educators as a way to help teachers add to their knowledge of books, as well as to build their classroom libraries.

Additionally, we recommend reviewing awarded books, such as those described in Appendix D. Each year, multiple books are submitted for consideration for all of these awards. Teams of educators, librarians, and readers review these books and select the awards. We also recommend checking books that might not have won an award but were given an honorable mention.

An Internet search will pull up many other book lists, including the New York Public Library's 100 Great Children's Books. Reviewing these lists provides a way to make sure that the classroom library is diverse in representation, genre, and reading level.

What Kids Select for Themselves and Other Kids to Read

One of the first places we look is the Children's Book Council, which sponsors the Children's and Teen Choice Book Awards. These awards are given to children's books by a panel of children.

Then there are the books that do not win awards but are wildly popular with children. These are the books that kids want to read—and adults sometimes discourage them from reading. Consider *Dogman* (Pilkey, 2016), the book series that has fantastic storylines about animals fighting crime. In Appendix E, we have listed some of the most popular series books.

We recommend seeing what all the fuss is about. Read one of the books. We continue to meet teachers who have been teaching for a long time who tell us, "Oh, my students read those books all the time, but I've never read one." In numerous instances, teachers tell us that after they read one, they were able to understand (even if they didn't personally like them), why their students liked them, and they were able to share a connection with one or several students around a shared joke.

The books that are wildly popular with kids are often part of a series. This delights children, and they often devour all of the books in the series, while parents and teachers wish their readers would find something else to read. However, before criticizing these books for their repetitive plots, consider that they offer comprehension support in the form of familiar characters and familiar types of problems. The books do not require as much mental energy to understand once one grasps the repeating elements from book to book. The familiarity and repetition can provide important support for reluctant readers or readers who may have limited vocabularies. Further, in series books students find familiar companions. They are comforted knowing what will happen without knowing all the details. The experience is not unlike the adult who binges on a Netflix series and may rewatch favorite episodes or even the entire season.

At the same time, we recognize the challenge of motivating students to read beyond their favorite series. Many libraries and websites have "If you liked _____, then try _____" to encourage students to try a different series. This attempt is often most successful if students make the recommendations.

See Appendix E for popular series books and Appendix G for Children's and Teen Choice Book Awards.

TEACHING COMPREHENSION IS FOR ALL STUDENTS

It may be easier to understand how to use a variety of authentic books with efficient readers. But what about those readers who struggle to read even the simplest texts? The reality is that most often they are given decodable texts (e.g., *The cat sat on the mat*). Many curricula suggest that readers need this kind of practice until they build up a foundation of word recognition and decoding skills. Only *after* they have this foundation, should more authentic books be used.

We challenge this sequential philosophy of reading. Will students need some practice time with decodable books? Probably. But they also need multiple opportunities to enjoy authentic books with enjoyable stories. The response to such a statement is, "But they can't read those texts!" We have used wordless books and Reader's Theater to address this challenge.

Wordless Books

In teaching comprehension, we encourage the use of wordless books. Someone is saying, "But they don't have any words!" Exactly! These books offer students of many levels and language abilities the opportunities to do the work of comprehension without the burdens of decoding. For example, when reading a wordless book, students can make connections with other pages in the book or with other books and experiences. They can make inferences, ask questions, and summarize what has happened. Wordless books that are good for making inferences include the following:

- *Tuesday* (Wiesner, 1991)
- *Flotsam* (Wiesner, 2006)
- *The Umbrella* (Schubert & Schubert, 2011)
- *Journey, Quest, and Return:* a trilogy of connected books by Becker (2013, 2014, and 2015)
- *Wave* (Lee, 2008)
- *The Only Child* (Guojing, 2015)
- *The Arrival* (Tan, 2007)
- *Chalk* (Thomson, 2010)

Readers' Theater

For Readers' Theater that helps focus on sense making, we "write" our own scripts, but follow an authentic children's literature text. We use the following procedures:

1. We decide in advance how many students will be in a group. Next, we decide on a text that is a little more advanced than what they can read on their own. Then, we type the lines from the book so that each student gets approximately the same amount of text to read. Instead of assigning parts, we make each person a narrator. (See Figure 5.2 for an example.)

2. We highlight each student's part before we give it to him or her. Over time, students take on this responsibility.

3. We start by reading the whole story and showing the pictures. This reading is just for fun and to familiarize them with the story.

4. Next, we read from our scripts. We usually have the picture book open in front of us and turn the pages as they read. Students sometimes use pictures for support.

5. We have students pause and think about the voices. We ask something like "What is Mother thinking? How does she sound in your mind? How would the mama sound? What is Father thinking? How would he sound?" Of course, we all pause to practice, but the speaker gets to decide the voice for that line. The benefit of having students take turns as narrators is that they typically get to change their voices. This isn't just for fun. It allows us to think about and voice

---

Narrator 1: Froggy woke up. It was freezing outside!

Narrator 2: Froggy yelled, "Snow! Snow! I want to play in the snow!"

Narrator 3: "Go back to sleep, Froggy. Frogs are supposed to sleep all winter," said Froggy's mother.

Narrator 4: "Wake up again when the snow melts," said Froggy's father.

Narrator 1: "No! No! I'm awake! I want to go out and play in the snow!" called Froggy.

Narrator 2: So Froggy put on his socks—zoop!

Narrator 3: Pulled on his boots—zup!

Narrator 4: Put on his hat—zat!

FIGURE 5.2. Readers' Theater using *Froggy Gets Dressed* (adapted from London, 1992).

how the characters are feeling and thinking (comprehension). Additionally, it gives us authentic reasons to read and reread the lines, building familiarity with words that these students might not otherwise encounter.

6. We have them partner with one other person and practice reading just their parts.

7. We have them read their parts individually, reading out loud and choosing what kind of voice they want to use. As necessary, we help them practice appropriate phrasing so that they understand and communicate the meaning.

8. We do another run-through—standing this time—as our dress rehearsal.

9. Depending on time and need, we go through sections again or have students practice just their lines. Sometimes we have them choose one or two lines and add a gesture that helps them show the audience part of the meaning (a shrug to show that the character is confused or an eye roll to show frustration).

10. Performance! The key to enjoyment and helping students have tolerance for repeated practice is performance. Performance can happen on the same day, or the whole schedule can be spread out over 2 or 3 days. During the performance, we always show the pictures to the audience in case some of the students performing aren't understood. In that way, we make sure that the audience can comprehend what's happening without interrupting the performers.

The book and scripts were placed into a special tub of "Readers' Theater books," and students could read them when they had free reading time. They often chose to form a group to practice the script again. In this way, all students were given authentic texts to work with. Even students who hadn't been in the original group and who couldn't read all the words initially now knew the stories well enough to go through the texts on their own.

Our instructional practices emphasize helping students comprehend text. Sometimes students do not understand that comprehending is the point of reading. They may believe that knowing all the words, reading fast, or sounding fluent are all it takes to read well. Implementing theories such as adaptive teaching and GRR requires teachers who have a deep knowledge of their students and of books in order to move comprehension beyond a static set of strategies.

PRACTICE

Helping students to understand and engage meaningfully with the books they read requires an adaptive and flexible approach to the ways in which you use theories, materials, and resources. There are no set instructional practices or "right" theories. Rather, to support student comprehension, teachers should use their knowledge of students, of books, and of practice.

ACTIVITY 1. *Questions for Reflection*

1. What have you observed about students' understanding of reading? Does their understanding include ideas about why comprehension is a vital part of reading?

2. Describe a time when a teacher was adaptive to your own needs or when you have observed or implemented adaptive teaching.

ACTIVITY 2. *Digging Deeper*

Focus on an award given to children's literature or on a particular author. Find out all that you can about the award or the author. How might this knowledge shape your instruction with students?

ACTIVITY 3. *Case Study*

As the third-grade reading group began, Laura introduced the objective: "I can figure out what the main idea is in informational text." She reviewed the concepts of main idea and supporting details. She then told students that she was going to model how she used clues in the text to identify the main idea. She read and thought aloud. The modeling took 10 minutes, and students began to get restless as Laura talked through the entire article. When she reflected on her teaching, Laura commented, "Ugh, I talked too much. The kids were over it."

In Laura's case, her initial instruction followed the curriculum and staff expectations. She provided a clear objective and modeled identifying the main idea, guiding students from being observers to participants in an effort to scaffold their thinking. It was obvious that she was working very hard. At the same time, she was uncomfortable with the students' affect, which showed low engagement. They responded when they were asked to respond but little else. The students also spent little time reading, usually less than 5 minutes. Over time, Laura began to change her instructional method. She continued to use the core curriculum for limited lessons, but she began to introduce inquiry units into literacy instruction.

She felt constrained by the literacy core curriculum, which her team members used to plan grade-level units of instruction. As an avid reader herself, she was particularly passionate about trying to find more time for students to enjoy texts and read more books. These experiences strengthened her vision to provide her current students with more choices in what they read and more time to spend reading rather than practicing literacy activities, such as strategies, in isolation.

Laura's negotiation of expectations included looking carefully at team planning and noting when particular weeks were identified as "free" weeks in the calendar, either because the school week was shortened or because she wanted to schedule particular stories and units for specific weeks in the year. Additionally, she began shortening the time she spent on a core program story to 3 or even 2 days a week. With these adaptations, she was able to implement what she initially thought of as mini-inquiry projects for her students.

For example, in the weeks before Presidents' Day, she checked out and purchased approximately 60 books about U.S. presidents and the White House. Students first spent time reading books. As Laura noted, "It was silent in my classroom; kids were so engrossed in reading." During the reading periods in these designated days, students worked in small groups, taking notes on what they found interesting. Sometimes they worked independently but side by side so that they could share information. At other times, they worked collaboratively. Laura noted, "The students are talking to one another and they want to read, even those who read at a lower reading level." During the entire process, she asked them to consider how they could share the information they were learning with others.

When students had collected numerous facts, she asked that they work collaboratively with their group members to categorize them. These facts were grouped into categories, such as "The White House," "White House Ghosts," "Abraham Lincoln," and more. Students continued to read to search for more information to add to these categories or discard certain categories and add new ones.

Ultimately, students created PowerPoints to share their information. During a visit to Laura's classroom, we talked with students in each group. During that time, we did not observe a single student who was unable to tell us about the information they'd read. Toward the end of the hour-long visit, Laura stood in the center of the room in case students had questions, but students barely glanced at her. They worked with a clear purpose, spending lots of time reading and sharing with one another.

Laura's grade-level team showed interest in her inquiry projects, and together they implemented another inquiry unit on dangerous animals, suspending at least some of the reading programs. While Laura focused on helping her students meet the standards within the CCSS, as well as a deeper engagement with texts, other teachers felt that they should use the traditional unit reading tests that were part of their core reading program. One teacher expressed genuine surprise that her students' scores were higher than usual for the traditional reading test, even after skipping some of the traditional activities in order to conduct their own inquiry projects. Laura reflected that through inquiry:

> "We are meeting multiple goals that the team members and curriculum say I should be meeting, such as using text features, but this inquiry also supports important skills that aren't coming up in curriculum and our team meetings—things like meeting technology goals. And, students are more engaged than usual."

Consider:

- How did Laura's vision shape her teaching?

- How did Laura support her students' comprehension?

- Describe your experiences with curricular, school, and district expectations. How have you navigated these pressures to align with your vision?

ACTIVITY 4. *Using Children's Literature*

In order to support comprehension, students need to be able to make inferences. Teachers often model making inferences through their read-alouds. However, sometimes students do not need explicit modeling; instead, they need someone to name what they can already do.

Mr. Jones chose an alternative method for introducing inferences. He chose *Chalk* (Thomson, 2010), a wordless book. Instead of starting at the beginning, he chose a page approximately two-thirds of the way through where the shadow of a dinosaur falls across three children. Showing the image on the document camera, he follows three steps:

- He asks students to describe what they see. He lists their answers on the board under the heading "What we see." This list helps students focus on what is there. Ultimately, he will connect their list to a list of the evidence from the text.

- Next, he asks students to describe what might have happened to lead up to this picture. He writes their answers under the heading "Inferences." When students run out of ideas, he shows them the title of the book, *Chalk*, and prompts students by asking, "Does this title make you change or add to your inferences?"

- He asks students why they made the inferences that they did. He prompts them to think about other books that they're read or other movies they've seen, for example. This allows him to better understand what sources the students are connecting with in order to make inferences.

Following these three steps, he begins showing pictures from the beginning of the book. At this point, he does not narrate what is happening. Instead, he lets students think about the pictures on their own. Before he gets to the page he showed his students, he pauses once or twice and asks them if they would like to add to or change their inferences.

Mr. Jones uses this approach to helping his students understand how to make inferences as an anchor experience. Over time, he will ask them to make inferences when reading different texts, including the process of making hypotheses in science texts. He will help students understand that the process of making inferences is not about having the "correct" inference but of constantly adjusting their inferences as more information is revealed.

CHAPTER 6

How Can We Encourage Students to Read Widely?

WHAT'S THE BIG IDEA?

Students need to read widely. By reading widely, we mean that students need to read lots of books, read books from across different genres, and read for extended periods of time. In addition to seeing themselves represented in texts and appreciating viewpoints different from their own, as discussed in Chapter 4, reading widely is a critical component of purposeful teaching. Reading widely helps improve students' mental representations of texts and make sense of multiple kinds of books and documents. For example, as adults, we know that a contract is much different than a novel. Reading only novels does not prepare us to read and understand the fine print of legal documents. Reading widely builds our vocabulary and allows for readers to transition from one genre to another. Reading widely can also help us build our reading stamina, sustaining our reading over long periods of time.

However, the truth is that many of our students do not read widely, or even like to read. Some students read the same book over and over rather than venturing into an unknown series of books. Yet others prefer to read only graphic novels in which the main characters look like themselves and experience the same tribulations as they do (e.g., *Smile* [Telgemeier, 2010], *New Kid* [Craft, 2019], and *Invisible Emmie* [Libenson, 2017]). But why? Possible reasons for this include motivation, agency, and opportunities to read. Next, we discuss the theories that clarify why reading widely is important and how to encourage wide reading and consider practical ways to help our students read widely.

WHAT ARE THE THEORIES?

While the need to read widely might seem like common sense, it is also a position that is well supported by theory. In this section, we consider opportunity to read as a theory, as well as the potential that the opportunity to read has to increase student motivation to read and student agency (see Figure 6.1).

Opportunity to Read

Guthrie, Schafer, and Huang (2001) defined *opportunity to read* as instances when students encounter connected texts and have some responsibility for these encounters. Opportunity to read is influenced by multiple factors, including those that teachers have some influence over (time, text, and task) and those factors that students bring to the reading, including engagement and reading proficiency (Hiebert & Martin, 2009). Reading instruction in classrooms has long been criticized for keeping students at word-level tasks for a much greater percentage of the time than at text-level tasks (Brenner, Hiebert, & Tompkins, 2009). This is problematic, for as Hiebert and Martin (2009) pointed out:

> In any domain one can identify, whether it be a medical diagnosis, flying an aircraft, or programming computers, it would be absurd to think one becomes proficient without participating extensively in the activity, whether it be diagnosis, flying, or programming. When it comes to teaching students to read in schools, however, little attention is paid to the amount that students read texts. (pp. 3–4)

When students have multiple opportunities to read, they have multiple chances to get better at reading connected text. They also begin to develop expertise in choosing their own books and read more extensively than those students who are focused on word-level tasks (Hiebert & Martin, 2009). Opportunities to read connected text are correlated with increased fluency, vocabulary, and

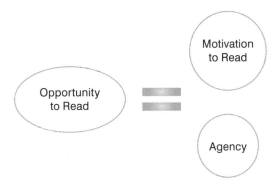

FIGURE 6.1. Opportunity to read.

comprehension (Brenner et al., 2009). Studies of effective literacy teachers have confirmed that a core practice was extensive time for students to read connected texts, as well as having access to literally hundreds of books (Allington & Johnston, 2002; Cunningham & Allington, 2015).

At issue is not simply that students should read more. While reading more is critical, reading more with comprehension helps create stamina for reading, something Hiebert (2014) labeled a forgotten reading proficiency. In a study of third graders, Brenner et al. (2009) found that students spent just 18 minutes of a 90-minute reading block reading connected text to themselves. This was more time than had been reported in previous studies, but certainly not close to the 90-minutes designated reading time students should read per day recommended to maintain their reading levels (Allington, 2012)

As Hiebert (2014) observed, the issue for many of our students is not that they can't identify words and understand most of the words they read; rather, they are not proficient at sustaining their focus on the text for extended periods of time. One way to combat this concern is through the use of interesting and engaging texts. The key to supporting students who read broadly is choice. Certainly, students need to be asked to read within genres they might not otherwise try. At the same time, researchers repeatedly confirm that students want choices about what to read (Allington & McGill-Franzen, 2018; Zumbrunn et al., 2019).

We also need to recognize that reading is not limited to cognitive responses. Rosenblatt (1994) noted that reading is guided not just by the reader's intellect, but also by an emotional response. Emotional responses serve as more than just a foundation for enjoyment and motivation. Lysaker, Tonge, Gaulson, and Miller (2011) used children's literature, specifically narratives, to help support students' social interactions with others. Their study suggested that readers can learn more about how to live within the world by understanding how characters feel, act, and relate to one another. "The role of story in human experience suggests that story influences the development of certain relational capacities . . . stories provide relational contexts within which we are asked to imagine the motivations and actions of others, which leads to enhanced social imagination (Lysaker et al., 2011, p. 531). With focused instruction, these researchers concluded that "children took up the identity of the characters as some aspects of themselves, which had the effect of developing their intimate knowledge of others through the internalized comingling of the voices of reader and text" (p. 552).

Motivation

Motivation theory supports wide reading. Multiple definitions of *motivation* exist. Jang, Conradi, McKenna, and Jones (2015) related motivation specifically to reading when they defined the concept as what *moves* students to pick up a book (or a magazine or a device) and what *moves* students to persist in reading that text, even when it might become challenging or boring" (p. 240). Other theories of motivation include Guthrie and Wigfield's (2000) engagement model of reading, which highlights that "engaged reading is motivated, strategic, knowledge-driven, and socially interactive" (p. 404). They continue, such students are "motivated to read, strategic in their approaches to comprehending what they read, knowledgeable in their construction of meaning from text, and socially interactive while reading" (Guthrie, Wigfield, & You, 2012, p. 602).

Why is motivation so important? Knowing how to read and understand texts is not the same as being motivated to read the text. Motivation to read is linked to increased achievement (Gambrell, 2011; Malloy et al., 2017). It is also what keeps students reading over time, allowing them to develop content knowledge and pursue their own interests and goals.

How is motivation developed? We know that there are a variety of factors that influence motivation. Attitudes toward reading and the value of reading are important components of motivation. Positive attitudes and valuing reading are not either/or factors. Instead, they can be developed with time through ongoing positive interactions with texts (Jang et al., 2015). This means that students need multiple exposures to texts, numerous opportunities to choose their own texts, and ongoing time to dialogue with others. Gambrell (2011) summarized seven practices that support students' motivation:

- Reading tasks and activities that are relevant to their lives
- Access to a wide range of materials
- Opportunities for sustained reading
- Choices in what they read and what tasks they complete
- Social interaction around texts
- Challenging texts and the necessary scaffolds to be successful in the challenging texts
- Rewards and incentives for reading are not extrinsic but are linked to the value of reading

Motivation is not solely the domain of an individual. Although motivation influences and is influenced by a student's identity and learning, something researchers have termed "intertwining" (Nasir, 2002; Nasir & Cooks, 2009), motivation also has a social component. Students may be motivated to learn in order to participate in a community of practice that is part of their desired identity. The authors of *How People Learn II* (National Academies of Sciences, Engineering, and Medicine, 2018) concluded that "motivation to learn is fostered for learners of all ages when they perceive the school or learning environment is a place where they 'belong' and when the environment promotes their sense of agency and purpose" (pp. 5–6).

Related to reading, we sometimes observe this interplay of individual motivation and social interaction among our students. Perhaps you remember when the newest Harry Potter book was released. We recall first- and second-grade students carrying around books that were a hefty 3 inches thick. Although some of them were not able to read the majority of the words in a single paragraph, they desperately wanted to be a part of the "community" that was Harry Potter Readers. This example illustrates how powerful a community can be. At the same time, it is important to note that it is not simply participation in a random group that provides the motivation; rather, it is participation in a community that is desired by the individual.

Agency

Agency is another critical dimension of wide reading and refers to an individual's ability to intentionally influence thoughts and actions. An agentic individual exercises "desire, ability, and power to determine their own course of action" (Vaughn, 2018, p. 63). Developing a sense of agency allows individuals to author new identities (Tan, Barton, Kang, & O'Neill, 2013). In terms of reading, taking on an agentic stance affords readers the power to make decisions and choices and to influence their learning context. Johnston emphasizes the important role of agency regarding literacy context:

> If nothing else, children should leave school with a sense that if they act, and act strategically, they can accomplish their goals. Having a sense of agency then is fundamental. Our well-being depends on it. Children with a strong belief in their own agency work harder, focus their attention better, are more interested in their studies, and are less likely to give up when they encounter difficulties than children with a weaker sense of agency (Johnston, 2004, pp. 29, 30, 41).

Student agency is often considered an important dimension of literacy learning. When students make decisions that show they are in charge of their learning, they become active members of the learning community. In a review of exemplary first- and fourth-grade teachers, Pressley, Allington, Wharton-McDonald, Block, and Morrow (2001) found that learning contexts in which students harnessed their agency began making more independent decisions as readers and writers than students in more restrictive learning contexts. In fact, Pressley and colleagues (2001) found that "we observed teachers . . . insisting students actually read books they chose . . . and the most effective teachers did more to encourage students to do things for themselves than did least effective teachers" (pp. 14, 17). This means that students need opportunities to make decisions about what they read, challenge and ask questions about what they read, and interact with texts on their own terms. In our research, we have found the following practices necessary to support students' agency in the context of reading:

- Access to make decisions about texts
- Opportunities to choose the types of tasks they complete

- Support to persist when tasks are challenging
- Opportunities to interact with others
- Intentions and ideas are scaffolded

For example, in one third-grade classroom, students harnessed their agency, and their teacher, Ms. Callie, helped sustain their efforts with the following instructional supports. Ms. Callie works with her students to help them find the texts connected to their research topics. Students select their favorite books and post these recommendations for others to read. Continually, Ms. Callie has discussions with her students about their interests and encourages her students to talk with one another about what they read (Vaughn, Premo, Sotirovska, & Erickson, 2020).

In classrooms where students have agency and decision-making power, they have responsibility for what they read. Such contexts are essential when it comes to developing purposeful teaching opportunities for students to enjoy reading and develop the necessary skills to become successful in reading.

PRACTICAL CONSIDERATIONS

How Do You Connect Students to Texts?

Practically speaking, how can teachers connect students to texts? We divide these text encounters into three broad categories: times when the teacher introduces the students to particular books, structured opportunities to read, and independent opportunities to read. Students benefit from a steady blend of all three types of text encounters.

Introducing Students to Books

Read-Alouds

As educators, we spend a lot of time talking with students. One question we like to ask students is to describe a time when they enjoyed reading. The most common responses include a read-aloud by a family member, friend, or teacher. While read-alouds can help students learn content, we emphasize that at least some read-aloud times should be for pleasure only. Introducing books should include sharing them for the sake of promoting a love of reading. This can happen with all students of all grade levels. For example, when working with middle school readers who are not on grade level, we begin by sharing a favorite book and promising that we would not ask them to summarize, make connections, or name a character. They can ask questions if they want to, but we do not require them to do any "academic" task with the text. This practice allows students who have experienced repeated failures with readings to connect with a text in a different way than they had recently experienced in school.

Read-alouds can be used to entice students to read. One fourth-grade teacher we know makes it his practice to read several books from different series to his students. However, he only reads the first book of the series to his class and leaves the rest of the series available for students to read on their own.

Book Talks

Marinak and Gambrell (2016) recommend using a "bless this book" time, in which teachers instill a passion for books by blessing the book and encouraging students to read the texts that are blessed. Students can join in on this process by doing their own "bless this book" in the classroom. Students select books of interest and recommend them to others in their classrooms and in the rest of the school. As mentioned in the earlier example, Ms. Callie builds on this idea by posting students' recommendations outside of her classroom where members of the school community can see these recommendations.

Structured Opportunities to Read

Book Clubs and Literature Circles

Book clubs or literature circles vary by name, but ideally are linked by student ownership and book choice. They differ from small groups, often referred to as guided-reading groups where the teacher leads students through a shared text. In book clubs or literature circles, the teacher may serve as a facilitator or co-member of the group. However, the ultimate goal is for the students to assume the leadership of their group. Student choice is essential to book clubs or literature circles. Daniels (2002) noted, "In traditional American schools, virtually every single book, article, story, text, poem, chapter, novel, and play that students read throughout their first 12 or 13 years is assigned by a teacher, dictated by the curriculum, and backed by the authority of grades" (p. 20).

By offering students a range of choices to select from, as well as a range of ways to share what they have read about, students have multiple opportunities to interact meaningfully with texts and with one another. See Appendix F for books that are popular book club choices.

Author Studies

Author studies are an approach to learning about books in which students can work as a class, in small groups, or individually. Students can make connections between the author's works and life and learn about his or her writing style. As a result, students can make connections between the author's experiences and life events and the characters and themes in a story as well as improving their critical thinking skills across texts. Author studies typically involve reading several books by an author, conducting research on the author, and analyzing the books read with the aim of building toward a culminating project.

Set goals for the author study, and think critically about what authors you are introducing and for what purpose. Before you plan an author study, answer the following questions:

- What is the function and purpose for an author study in your classroom?
- What authors do you want to include and why?
- How will you structure the author study?

Independent Opportunities to Read

Independent opportunities to read are created when students are able to read a variety of books of their choice. When students have perceived control and autonomy over the types of texts they read, they are more willing to read throughout the day.

Students choose their own books for *sustained silent reading* (SSR; Reutzel, Fawson, & Smith, 2008). How do students choose appropriately challenging texts? Many teachers find the five-finger rule helpful. This strategy involves having students read the first page, and if they come across five words that are unknown, they choose a different book. However, free reading time is not an opportunity for teachers to remain inactive. For example, *scaffolded sustained silent reading* (ScSR; Reutzel, Fawson, & Smith, 2008) is scaffolded instruction during SSR, in which teachers can model fluent reading before the class embarks on their reading, students monitor what they read to ensure that they read books in different genres, and teachers conduct brief reading conferences to discuss text selection and overall comprehension.

Scaffolded Sustained Silent Reading

1. *Access.* Plan how students will access books by creating clear categories of texts, such as by genre. Create an accountability sheet that helps students read a selection of texts from different categories.
2. *Model.* Teach students how to select books and evaluate if a text is appropriate for them to read with fluency and understand without outside help.
3. *Evaluate.* As students read, conference with them. Ask them to read a paragraph or retell part of what they have read. Evaluate students' progress based on fluency and comprehension. Reteach strategies as needed.
4. *Book projects.* When students finish their books, they share them with the rest of the class through teacher-directed or student-created options.

We recognize the challenge that finding independent reading time poses to teachers, so we offer a few practical suggestions to consider when thinking if it might be possible in your classroom:

- *Start small.* Look for a 15–20 minute block for older readers or one 5–10 minute block for younger readers once during the quarter.
- *Ask the students.* Talk to them about your plan and ask them to help you think about when time could be scheduled.
- *Start a lunch bunch.* Instead of starting with the whole class, invite students who are interested to join you for a reading lunch once a month.

Supporting students' reading of multiple texts over extended periods of time isn't only common sense. It is documented by many theories that connect wide reading to students' achievement, motivation, social and emotional awareness, and empathy. Encouraging students to read widely requires purposeful planning, a wealth of books, and creating space in a busy curriculum for students to enjoy the books.

PRACTICE

In order to encourage students to read widely, they must have a variety of opportunities to engage with authentic, culturally relevant, and meaningful texts. Teachers should consider the roles of motivation and agency and how the classroom is structured to support opportunities to read.

ACTIVITY I. *Questions for Reflection*

1. Choose one of the theories (opportunity to read, motivation, or agency) and describe why it is important to help students read widely.

2. Describe how this chapter answers "How do you encourage students to read widely?" What other ways have you observed students being encouraged to read widely that are not mentioned?

ACTIVITY 2. *Scaffolding for Success with Literature Circles and Book Clubs*

1. If students are unfamiliar with the format, select a short story or shared book for the whole class to read. Divide students into groups, or let students select their groups. Create one or two questions that each group will discuss. Allow time for students to read and to talk. Share with the whole class how groups responded to the questions. Ask students to reflect on the process of talking in groups and how they could help groups run more smoothly.

2. Next, students make their top selections, and the teacher helps to facilitate literature circles. Help students establish norms for their group. For example, will students read the material before coming to the group? What happens when someone hasn't read the material? What will they talk about in the group? Should they write an exit ticket or list to show what they talked about?

3. When students are ready for more independence, focus on a theme or general topic. Gather numerous books that connect to the theme, and ask students to vote for their top three or four books. Students then pick their top two choices from the narrowed list.

4. Some teachers find that providing roles for students is a helpful tool to ensure that all students participate in the discussion. Possible roles include:

   - *Discussion director:* creates two or three questions to help guide the group's discussion about the text.
   - *Word detective:* records new or interesting words from the selection.
   - *Connector:* selects significant sections of the text and draws connections to real life.
   - *Summarizer:* prepares a brief summary of what has happened in the text so far.
   - *Investigator:* researches background information that may help the group understand the text, including finding out information about geographical locations, historical events, or the author's writing style.

   Although these roles are helpful in launching literature circles, teachers should decrease their use of them as students become more skilled in their discussions of books.

5. Scaffold student talk as necessary. We have seen teachers use the following techniques to scaffold students during literature circles. Ask students to plan a final project for sharing their books with the whole class or possibly a broader audience. Students might list ideas, and everyone can choose from the list. Final projects create opportunities for extending the conversations about books and for making decisions about what to do and how to do it. Final projects allow students to summarize what they've learned as well as think about how to encourage others to read the book. Students can act out a key scene, write a fan-fiction piece, video a BookTube review, or write to the author.

6. Some things to consider:

   - Don't be afraid to let students read books at more advanced levels. When offering books for students to choose from, select a variety of levels. However, let students choose the book for themselves. If they choose a book that is advanced, it is up to the group members to support each other. If they choose a book that is easy for them, it may give them more time to focus on written responses.

- When groups run into difficulty, invite the whole class to problem-solve, rather than trying to solve the problem for them. Imagine that a group is off task. Solicit ideas from the whole class about possible solutions. Let the group pick one or two ideas and try them out, then report back on how the process went.
- Encourage students to reflect on the process of selecting the book for their book club, as well as what they learned from the activity. Was the book too hard? Too easy? What kind of book do they think would be good to read the next time?

Evaluating Book Clubs

A critical component of book clubs is accountability. Although the teacher might not be directly involved in each group on a daily basis, specific structures for evaluation should be in place. Accountability should provide information about students' reading (decoding, fluency, and comprehension), students' awareness of their own thinking during reading, and how students are functioning as a group.

We like to use an observation sheet and watch student groups (see Figure 6.2). When checking student responses, we hope that the responses show that students will be able to move beyond summarizing and describing favorite parts and begin to focus on the elements that we have been teaching, such as the author's craft, tone, and theme, elements of the argument, connections to the larger world, and more. We match this component to the instruction that we have already given in the classroom.

In addition to using our own observation sheet, we ask students to evaluate themselves. Student self-assessment is a particularly vital part of accountability, feedback, and developing their agency as readers. Black and Wiliam's (1998) extensive review of classroom assessment literature determined that self-assessment is part of the feedback loop that can raise students' academic performance as well as their self-esteem—what Afflerbach and Meuwissen (2005) described as their "sense of self as a reader" (p. 145). As students take responsibility for their own assessment, they are more likely to attribute success to their own effort, resulting in increased motivation to read.

Finally, we evaluate their final projects. We invite students to help us create criteria and a rubric for final projects. We suggest criteria to consider, such as "shows others what the book is about but doesn't give away the whole story."

ACTIVITY 3. Case Study

In this case study, we share how we incorporate authentic and engaging literature into our work with students.

Book club elements	Evidence
Students came to the book club prepared.	
Students shared their ideas and listened to one another (speaking and listening).	
Students were able to move beyond summarizing and listing their favorite parts of the book and to consider _____.	
Other:	

FIGURE 6.2. Assessment for book clubs.

Margaret routinely works with third-to-fifth graders, conducting after-school book clubs. A central part of the after-school book club experience is student choice. Students are free to select any text they want based on their interests and are given a week's time frame to stop reading a book once the book clubs start. Students are asked to reflect on whether the books grab them and, if they don't, to abandon them. We often talk about how there are way too many interesting and good books to read—if a book is not interesting, feel free to pick another one. Before the book clubs start, Margaret invites students to talk about their reading lives. She asks them to complete a handout in which they answer the following questions:

- When you find books that are interesting to you, what do they tend to be like?
- What should I know about books in your life?
- What do you not like about reading? Why?
- What do you want to tell me about yourself as a reader?

Dixie spends the summer working with students who have been identified as needing additional help with reading. Many of them are initially resistant to reading. Instead of beginning with assessments to identify their reading levels, Dixie begins with observations of and interviews with her students. Like the questions listed on Margaret's handout, the interviews focus on their interests and reading lives.

At the same time, Dixie reads aloud every day from books such as *The Crossover* (Alexander, 2014). Students are typically surprised by the time spent reading aloud, yet the read-aloud time is consistently voted among the favorite activities of the summer experience. She purposefully selected the book because of its authentic portrayal of African American middle school students. Additionally, this text works well because it is a connected story written in free verse. The fact that many pages have very few words on them makes the book less intimidating to students who are hesitant to read on their own. Finally, the story line of the book is continued in a prequel (*Rebound* [Alexander, 2018]) that students can continue reading on their own, as well as books with a similar topic and format written by the same author.

Finally, students are allowed to choose their own topics and to spend a portion of their time pursuing their own interests. At the end of the summer experience, students share what they've learned with their peers.

ACTIVITY 4. *Using Children's Literature*

Reflect on the questions about how Sam, who has taught fourth grade for 2 years, used multicultural literature and how it shaped his instruction.

- What are the important dimensions of Sam's vision?
- How did Sam structure his classroom to support spaces where students have opportunities to read, collaborate, and develop a sense of agency in their learning?

A Snapshot of a Classroom Using Author Study

Sam has a vision for teaching that involves developing students who have the power to see beyond where they currently are and to use reading as a tool to expand opportunities for themselves.

Sam invited his students to read texts by Faith Ringgold in his author study series. He purposefully chose this author because he wanted to include female authors of color and wanted to provide texts in which students could see themselves in what they read:

- *Tar Beach* (Ringgold, 1991)
- *We Came to America* (Ringgold, 2016)
- *Aunt Harriet's Underground Railroad in the Sky* (Ringgold, 1992)
- *If a Bus Could Talk* (Ringgold, 1993)
- *My Dream of Martin Luther King* (Ringgold, 1995)

Instructional Plan

1. Sam asked students to select the author they wanted to research and then, after the class was split into two groups, provided students with the following options to conduct their author study.

2. As a whole class, students read aloud each story and discussed important themes in the story.

3. Within their author study groups, students charted what the characters were doing in each text, and then compared and contrasted the characters' actions in the different books.

4. Students explored more about the historical events described in their individual books to better understand the characters.

5. Students listed the themes, voice, and style for their individual books, and then compared these elements across the books.

6. Students researched the life of their author and then created "Questions to Ask the Author" about his or her books. Students then came up with a way to share their information about the author with the class and/or the entire school.

CHAPTER 7

How Can We Incorporate Expository Text Purposefully?

WHAT'S THE BIG IDEA?

Purposeful teaching builds on using various types of literature to connect with students' experiences, their lives both in and out of school, and their interests. All genres provide opportunities for achieving this type of connection. However, expository text is a unique genre that can be used to engage students in connecting with the real world using relevant and accurate depictions of the world we live in. In this chapter, we focus on the important role of expository texts when using children's literature and structuring purposeful reading opportunities in classrooms.

WHAT ARE THE THEORIES?

Expository text is a particular type of text that informs and/or persuades the reader. Expository text can be particularly challenging for readers because it deals with unfamiliar content and because a variety of text structures are used to organize expository content (Williams, 2018). Further, many books for young children may be organized in ways that do not highlight the important text features needed to guide young readers in comprehending expository texts, which can be more complex than narrative texts.

Expository texts comprise a broad category (see Table 7.1), including texts that are nonfiction and informational, and that provide knowledge about a topic to the reader. Often, you hear the term informational text and expository text used interchangeably. This is understandable given that both types of texts convey

TABLE 7.1. Expository Text Formats

Format	Description	Examples
Cause–effect	Presents an event, or cause, as well as the effects that the event had.	Editorials, warning labels
Compare–contrast	Describes similarities and differences between events or concepts.	Sports article comparing and contrasting two teams; advertisements comparing and contrasting one item with another brand
Description	Describes a topic by listing characteristics and features.	Book about dogs; travel brochures
Problem–solution	Shows a problem and one or more solutions.	News report about climate change; primary document of a presidential speech
Chronological	Lists events in sequence or order.	Historical account of a famous person's life; steps to follow in a recipe

knowledge to the reader and provide facts about a particular topic or phenomenon. However, expository texts differ from informational texts in that expository texts can provide a certain perspective or opinion and also include facts and details, whereas informational texts solely provide facts and details.

Background Knowledge

The background knowledge that a reader brings to the text significantly influences comprehension (Caldwell & Leslie, 2012; Duke, Pearson, Strachan, & Billman, 2011). Prior experiences and exposure to the particular topic being described influences vocabulary knowledge (Stahl, Hare, Sinatra, & Gregory, 1991) and conceptual knowledge (Marzano, 2004). For example, consider a recent teaching experience we had with a group of fourth graders. While beginning a unit on immigration, these students were asked about recent immigration policies. Students were then asked to think about another time in history when immigration played a major role in shaping the U.S. workforce. For many of the students, immigration was not something they knew about firsthand—nor had they learned the information that over 40 million immigrants came to Ellis Island in 1892 through their social studies curriculum.

In other words, these students lacked the necessary background knowledge to make sense or comprehend an online article shared in class about the complexities of immigration policy. As they were reading the article about the past debate over building a wall to prevent immigrants from entering into the United States, they missed an important connection to the nation's history and lacked perspective about the topic. Without this pivotal background knowledge, students inadvertently held an uninformed view of the topic as it related to the teacher's goal of studying immigration policies in the United States.

As this example illustrates, background knowledge is essential in helping students to comprehend and to make inferences about what they are reading. "What students *already know* about the content is one of the strongest indicators of how well they will learn new information relative to the content" (Marzano, 2004, p. 1). In fact, scholars repeatedly emphasize the important role of background knowledge when developing students' comprehension of a particular topic (Guthrie, 2008). This background knowledge is vital in helping students make inferences, allowing them to read more challenging texts and contributing to deep comprehension (Wolf, 2018). Wolf (2018) noted, "The more we know, the more we can draw analogies, and the more we can use those analogies to infer, deduce, analyze, and evaluate our past assumptions—all of which increases and refines our growing internal platform of knowledge" (Ch. 3, "Analogy and Inference," paragraph 2, p. 36).

Background knowledge is important in both expository and narrative texts, but research suggests that it is particularly critical when making sense of expository texts. McNamara, Floyd, Best, and Louwerse (2004) asked third graders to read one narrative and one expository text and explored the different levels of comprehension. Comprehension of the expository text was significantly related to the students' background knowledge in ways that comprehension of the narrative text was not. In other words, students develop background knowledge and schemas about the particular topic or phenomenon that inform their ability to comprehend expository texts. Schemas help illuminate how readers can comprehend challenging texts through an interactive process, whereby students make connections with what they read based on background knowledge and the specific text they encounter (Herman, Anderson, Pearson, & Nagy, 1987).

Despite the important role of background or prior knowledge, we also know that it has been called a double-edged sword in serving as a beneficial influence on comprehension (Block & Pressley, 2002). For example, although prior knowledge can help with a student's understanding, it can also interfere with it (Massey, 2007), meaning that what a reader has experienced or thinks can hijack the understanding of the words on the page. Cameron's story (Massey, 2007) is one example of ineffective prior knowledge. Cameron was a third-grade reader who scored below benchmark levels on state assessments. His reading concerned his parents and teachers for many reasons, not the least of which was his continued failure to pass the quarterly tests that were indicative of the scores he could expect to receive on his reading test at the end of the year.

The pressure was on for Cameron to either pass the test or be retained. In working with Cameron, it became evident that he relied heavily on what he knew—or what he thought he knew. Repeatedly, he would read an excerpt from a text and say, "This is wrong," or "This isn't what the Discovery Channel said." Although the text Cameron read certainly wouldn't be the first one to give contradictory information, what Cameron thought he knew from a variety of sources was valued over what the text stated.

Like Cameron, as students are exposed to various forms of media in today's informational landscape, background knowledge based on media accounts is not always accurate and requires that teachers use expository texts as a tool to distinguish facts from fiction. But how do teachers use expository texts in a way that can effectively maximize the content, structure, purpose, and function of this particular genre? There are many approaches, but one that is helpful is teaching how expository texts are fundamentally different from narrative texts. In other words, their text structure is unique in comparison to other genres.

Text Structure

Text structure refers to the pattern of the text and is critical in helping to understand expository texts. Utilizing and understanding text structure improves the reading comprehension of expository text for readers at multiple levels (Hebert, Bohaty, Nelson, & Brown, 2016; Pyle et al., 2017). Meyer, Brandt, and Bluth (1980) discovered that students who were taught to attend to text structure and the accompanying signal words were able to recall important information after reading. Similarly, Duke et al. (2011) list text structure as one of the 10 elements of effective comprehension instruction. It signals the reader where to focus attention.

Many of us use text structure without being aware of it. If a story starts "long ago," we are likely to recognize it as a narrative structure. Narrative structure is very familiar to many children and adults, in part because of movies and television. However, expository patterns or structures are not always as familiar because they are varied (e.g., problem–solution, chronological, descriptive, and cause–effect) and frequently layered (e.g., a text can have a chronological and a problem-solution structure). Further, expository texts contain often highly specialized content focused on a particular topic. Consider the stats on a football card or a baseball card. These cards could be considered a very specific, specialized form of text. They have a structure that has meaning for some people, while others struggle to understand a single thing on the card.

Wijekumarn and Beerwinkle (2018) described the following text structures as helpful in understanding how to use expository texts:

- *Description:* The author describes the phenomenon or topic using facts and descriptions.
- *Sequence:* The author uses sequencing as a tool to convey information about the topic.
- *Compare–contrast:* The author uses a compare and contrast pattern to provide information about a topic usually using two or more topics or phenomena.
- *Problem–solution:* The author highlights a question or problem, then uses facts and information to answer the problem and find the solution.

In this way, a knowledge of text structure signals readers what to pay attention to as they read (Duke et al., 2011). Consider how we (yes, adults too rely on text structure, it's not just for elementary students) use knowledge of text structure within expository texts. For example, as we were writing this book after seeing the devastation of the forest fires in the Pacific Northwest, we looked further at reports about the average rainfall in the months of August and September to understand how and if the weather might shift to help with the ongoing conflagration. Although we are not foresters or meteorologists, and found much of the information about average rainfall and weather patterns challenging to understand, we knew as we began reading these documents the types of language patterns and text structures we'd encounter as we read: compare–contrast, sequence, and problem–solution.

In school, students might read a text on planets describing their individual characteristics and an opinion-based text about global climate change and its impact on the environment that has numerous facts to support the authors' arguments. Students would read each of these types of texts for different purposes. Students might read the first text to learn specific facts about the planets, whereas they might be reading the second text to learn about the critical impact and effect that climate change is having on planets (i.e., cause and effect) and using this information to develop their own opinion about global climate change.

Text features are an important part of text structure that help signal a text as expository and what kind of text structure is being used (see Table 7.2). For example, when we viewed texts about the wildfires and encountered graphs comparing the average rainfall this year with rainfall in the past 5 years, we knew that at least part of the text was written in a compare–contrast structure. This feature signaled to us that we needed to carefully consider what was the same and what was different from one year to the next. Other important text features that may help indicate what kind of text structure is being presented include headings and subheadings, photographs and captions, maps, time lines, bold words, and tables. These features can help the reader. They can also hinder comprehension if the reader fails to pay attention to them, if the feature doesn't correlate with the text (as when a photograph unrelated to the text is used), or if the reader is overwhelmed with graphic information and doesn't know where to focus his or her attention on the page.

Academic Vocabulary

Also crucial to comprehension of expository texts is the understanding of vocabulary and its role in expository texts. Academic vocabulary has gained renewed attention with the advancement of the CCSS, which emphasize the important role of academic vocabulary in supporting reading comprehension. However, a definition of academic vocabulary can be tricky. There is general agreement that

TABLE 7.2. Expository Text Features

Feature	What students might miss
Title and subtitles	Students may neglect to follow titles and subtitles that show them the author's organization or outline of the article.
Table of contents	Students may try to find information in the text by skimming the whole text instead of using the table of contents to focus their search.
Photographs and drawings with captions	Students may skip photographs, drawings, or captions. They may believe that the text conveys all of the meaning.
Index	Students may not be familiar with books that have an index. Students may try to find information they want by skimming the whole text.
Glossary	Students may not be familiar with books that have a glossary. They may simply skip unknown words.
Maps	Students may not understand why a map is important to the text, or they may not know how to read a map or the scale of the map.
Text boxes	Students may skip text boxes, especially if it is hard to determine a sequence that the text boxes should be read in, or students may struggle to focus if there are multiple text boxes.
Charts and graphs	Students may not understand how the chart or graph connects to the rest of the text. They may be unfamiliar with different types of charts and graphs.

students will need to know vocabulary from different domains of knowledge. Fisher and Frey (2008) organized words into three clusters: (1) *general words:* basic high-frequency words needed for reading; (2) *specialized words:* words that appear fairly frequently in different types of texts but whose meanings are discipline specific; and (3) *technical words:* discipline- or subject-matter-specific terms.

Expository text requires students to use all three of these clusters, with a particular emphasis on specialized words and technical words. Repeatedly, research documents that when students have a large repertoire of words, they are better equipped to handle and comprehend challenging texts (Stahl & Nagy, 2006). Further, "vocabulary becomes the information base from which students will make inferences by connecting to prior knowledge, whereby cumulative content learning outcomes are realized" (Heafner & Massey, 2012, p. x).

And the effects are cumulative. The more words one knows, the easier it is to learn additional words. The trend whereby the more words a student knows, the broader the vocabulary a student will acquire widens over a student's school career, creating a Matthew effect, wherein those who know a lot of words learn more words, whereas those who have a limited exposure to words fall further and further behind (Heafner & Massey, 2012). Teaching academic vocabulary in addition to building students' word knowledge is essential in supporting students from a variety of backgrounds (Cruz & Thornton, 2009; Epstein, 2009; Marzano, 2004; Ogle, Klemp, & McBride, 2007).

But the answer is not as simple as teaching students a specified number of words per day. Stahl and Nagy (2006) estimated that students need between 4 and 12 exposures to a word in order to learn what a word means. Thus, what is needed is consistent exposure to words in context. Specifically, research tells us that when students learn words in authentic contexts they are more likely to remember and understand words they are reading (Allen, 2006, 2007; Marzano, 2004). And this method of learning highlights the importance of expository texts in developing academic vocabulary.

Consider the following example. If a student encounters the word *lugubrious* in a story, the context clues or the pictures may help him or her understand that a lugubrious person is sad or down. Thus, the reader has contextual support and a schema that already provides for understanding what the word *sad* means. However, when a reader encounters the word *democratic*, textual clues may not be enough for the reader to differentiate between the Democratic Party and a democratic form of government, without a schema that allows the reader to contrast it with other forms of government. That is, understanding the meaning of *democractic* requires a broad knowledge of the concept and its many related words and associations. In other words, there is an intertwining of comprehension, vocabulary knowledge, and background knowledge (Allen, 2006, 2007; Beck & McKeown, 1991; Marzano, 2004; Stahl & Nagy, 2006) when we think about using expository texts in the classroom—all of which are significant in increasing and supporting purposeful reading opportunities.

Although we see more and more exposure to expository texts in classrooms, given the requirements of the CCSS (which emphasize the importance of exposing students to informational text, identifying text features, and building academic vocabulary), this phenomenon is relatively new. We must be diligent in incorporating expository texts in the classroom. We are reminded of how Duke (2000), in her pivotal work on the role of informational text in 20 first-grade classrooms with students of different socioeconomic backgrounds, found that on average students were exposed to less than 2 minutes per day of reading informational texts! Fortunately, this situation no longer exists, but ensuring that students read more expository texts requires careful consideration of the purpose and function of these texts in the classroom today.

PRACTICAL CONSIDERATIONS

How Can You Use Expository Texts Purposefully in the Classroom?

One of the most challenging issues in working with expository texts that teachers report is how to share them with students. While biographies and autobiographies lend themselves to more traditional sharing, such as read-alouds or book clubs, sharing many of the other text structures may be harder to do. Thus, one of the first considerations is how to read expository texts to and with students. We recommend grouping expository texts and sharing enough books within the group for students to become familiar with the format, content, or style. Texts may be grouped by topic (which we discuss a bit later in "Rethinking Text Sets" on pp. 91–92), text structure/format, or author. The benefits of sharing a group of expository texts about mummies, for example, include helping students acquire more background knowledge about a particular time, place, and topic, as well as gaining multiple exposures to academic vocabulary associated with the content. Grouping by text structure allows students to begin to internalize particular ways of communicating information.

Grouping expository texts by text structure might include sharing a collection of texts written in infographic form (e.g., *U.S. History through Infographics* [Kenney, 2014a], *Economics through Infographics* [Kenney, 2014b], and *The Infographic Guide to American Government* [Lytle, 2019]). Some books capitalize on time lines (e.g., DK's *When on Earth* [2015] and *Timelines of Everything* [2018]) that can be used in connection with texts that share one or two time lines. Other books can be grouped by author, so that students learn more about particular topics as well as the way an author's writing flows (e.g., Jerry Pallotta's [n.d.] alphabet books series about insects, butterflies, boats, and more; Morley's [n.d.] You Wouldn't Want to Be series that helps readers imagine living in particular times and places; or Basher's [2007, 2009] use of illustration and personification to make topics like the periodic table or rocks and minerals engaging for readers).

Teachers who regularly read expository texts embrace the contrasts they offer. For example, rather than reading a chapter for a specified segment of time, Ms. Shirley used expository texts to help students transition from seats to carpet. As students arrived at the carpet, they put a sticky note on the page they wanted Ms. Shirley to read from the collection of Steve Jenkins's books she kept by her chair. The students were especially captivated by the illustrations in *Actual Size* (Jenkins, 2011), and Ms. Shirley read and reread pages.

Students placed their own hands on the illustration depicting the gorilla's hand. Ms. Shirley understood that it didn't matter whether the text was read in order. She also understood that students were gaining important information about sizes and perspective. This knowledge helped students as they encountered a different text by the same author that compares and contrasts two things, *Hottest, Coldest, Highest, Deepest* (Jenkins, 2004). Other ways of sharing expository texts included sharing single pictures or single page spreads from expository graphic novels such as *Drowned City* (Brown, 2015), asking students to share an interesting fact from a sports almanac, or selecting a particular component, such as a time line or map, and creating a visual that is referenced throughout a unit. This type of sharing is best shown using a document camera or other device that allows students to see images as well as special text features of expository texts, such as charts and maps.

There are many different types of expository texts that students may encounter or may already be reading. Consider Cade. As a second grader, he was given his first pack of Pokémon cards at a birthday party. He regularly studied the cards and began collecting more. While looking for additional Pokémon cards, he discovered football cards. He taught himself what the abbreviations meant and learned to read information in chart format. He gained a great deal of mathematical knowledge, including an understanding of percentages, decimals, and rankings. Collecting football cards became a passionate interest of his. They served as a gateway to reading about football history, football players and franchises, and more. The next progression was to seek out the most current information about the sport, so that by sixth grade, Cade was choosing to read current magazines cover to cover that described the football drafts in 200-plus pages. Cade's actions mirror those of adult readers, who pursue topics of interest through print or digital periodicals.

Mr. Kline, in his kindergarten classroom, uses informational text to highlight for his students the prominent text features seen when reading informational text. He asks students to look carefully at each page to identify what the text feature is and why the author is sharing that particular text feature in the text to help us as readers. Or consider Ms. Pansom, a second-grade teacher, who uses *The Important Book* by Margaret Wise Brown (1949) to model to students how to comprehend and write expository texts. After teaching a unit on writing summaries based on reading informational texts and detailing how to read informational text by using text features, Ms. Pansom transitions students into writing facts about different everyday objects based on *The Important Book*. The connection between reading and writing is discussed further in Chapter 8, but we highlight this classroom example here to emphasize how expository texts connect with authentic and integrated reading and writing projects in the classroom.

SERIES OF INQUIRY PROJECTS

As we've previously indicated, many students may already be using expository texts to pursue topics of their own interest. The following three types of inquiry projects leverage this type of inquiry and bring it into the classroom to elevate students' knowledge of texts and topics and increase their motivation. For example, there are a variety of ways in which students can engage in inquiry projects, from having students read current events on local websites and write a paragraph about something that interests them, for example, or learn about and debate a topic of interest, using the knowledge they've gained about a topic. In the following sections, we outline some motivating practices that can be used with expository texts to encourage students to read for an authentic purpose in the classroom.

Project-Based Learning

Understanding the role of expository texts is important as you reflect on the tasks, texts, and the roles of readers. For example, one of the fifth-grade teachers with whom we work, Ms. Simms, engages her students in relevant learning opportunities by inviting them to create a list of interesting topics they want to research. She then works with her students to model how to use expository texts to engage in authentic learning to develop knowledge about their topic. Ms. Simms scaffolds her students' learning process by modeling the research process, conducting mini-lessons on how readers use different types of texts (i.e., primary documents, informational texts, and periodicals) to develop specialized knowledge about their topic. As students engage with using a variety of nonfiction texts, they experience firsthand reading for an authentic purpose. In this way, the use of expository texts in the classroom requires a careful consideration of the tasks, the type of texts, and the roles of the reader.

Project-based learning is a model of instruction that organizes learning around specific topics or projects (Duke, Halvorsen, & Strachan, 2016; Jones, Rasmussen, & Moffitt, 1997). Teachers create student-centered projects focused on an inquiry or on solving an authentic problem. Students are instrumental in the planning phases during project-based learning, and so too is understanding the importance of expository texts in supporting the inquiry process. For example, let's say your students express interest in researching the national parks. The driving question might be, how would students use expository texts to support learning and gain knowledge about the topic?

In Ms. Pruitt's fifth-grade class, in which students conducted this type of project-based learning unit, they were motivated to learn facts about the national parks. One of their guiding questions included: What are the important characteristics of the national parks? The students researched a variety of texts to develop specialized knowledge about the topic. They worked in small groups to document the characteristics. Each group approached the texts differently—one group focused on navigating the trails within the parks, another group discussed the results of deforestation on the parks, and yet another group examined the impact of tourism on the wildlife in the parks. As these various approaches suggest, students relied on reading informational texts about the parks, compiling and synthesizing learned information based on what they read, and engaging in authentic and relevant learning opportunities centered on their interests. Students were encouraged to come up with their specialized topic (i.e., trails, deforestation, and tourism). Project-based learning requires that students engage in meaningful and authentic learning experiences focused on reading, writing, discussing, and in this case, composing, for different purposes.

As students investigate and seek resolutions to problems, they acquire an understanding of key principles and concepts. Project-based learning also places students in realistic, contextualized problem-solving environments. In doing so, projects can serve to build bridges between phenomena in the classroom and real-life experiences; the questions and answers that arise in their daily enterprise are given value and are shown to be open to systematic inquiry. Project-based learning also promotes links among subject matter disciplines and presents an expanded, rather than narrow, view of subject matter. (Blumenfeld et al., 1991, p. 372)

Similarly, Duke (2016) outlines the important role of project-based learning in reading instruction, its connection to developing motivation and specialized content knowledge, and its relationship to student learning outcomes: "The more strongly the teachers implemented the [project-based learning] projects, the higher growth students made in informational reading and writing and in motivation" (p. 8).

Because the guiding question requires students to do research and then analyze and summarize their findings, a variety of primary resources and expository texts are essential in learning important details and facts as they pertain to the project's focus.

Genius Hour

Genius hour is a learning approach based on an idea adopted from Google, in which employees are allowed to work on an area of interest for a percentage of their overall time at work. The rationale is that if employees are allowed time to pursue their own interests, they would be more engaged and creative in the time they spent on work dedicated to the company's needs.

In the classroom, Genius hour is a good example of student-driven inquiry. Instead of the teacher choosing the topic, as in project-based learning, students can select their own topic (Fink, n.d.; Smith, 2017), and they are given time on a daily, weekly, or monthly basis to work on the topic they've chosen. They can work individually or collaboratively. Teachers put varying guidelines in place, depending on the age of the students (e.g., see West & Roberts, 2016, for Genius hour in kindergarten and Spencer, 2017, for Genius hour in eighth grade), but one critical feature is that students periodically share their inquiry progress. They may share a formal presentation through PowerPoint or another program, or may share the problems they encounter in their inquiry. The goal is for everyone in the room to be a learner and a teacher at the same time.

Dixie integrated Genius hour into summer school for struggling readers who were not at grade-level benchmarks (Lupo, Mitnick-Wilson, & Massey, 2016; Massey, 2015; Massey, Miller, & Metzger, 2017). Many students were initially reluctant to choose a topic or stated that they did not have anything they were interested in learning. However, interviews with students made it clear that they were not used to learning in this way and simply didn't know what to do or

where to start. They also struggled to get past the idea that the teacher had a particular answer or approach that they were supposed to find. Once they moved
past these notions, their research resulted in increased stamina for reading,
increased motivation to read, willingness to ask questions of other students and
teachers, and an increased sense of agency. For example, one student wanted to
research ferrets in order to convince his mom that a ferret would make a good pet
for their family. Another student wanted to learn to code. Still another student
wanted to learn more about his ancestral culture in Mexico. All of these students
could pursue their own topics at the same time. Instruction focused on finding
and evaluating sources and communicating the information to others.

Building Background Knowledge

In Chapter 4, we discussed the use of text sets to expose students to similar topics
and to explore themes across texts. We also shared that text sets enable us to for-
mulate an overarching concept using a variety of texts that are grouped together
around a particular concept. Here, we want to further develop the idea of text
sets and their relationship to the use of expository texts to build background
knowledge and to acquire the content knowledge and specialized vocabulary
often found in expository texts, which are particularly helpful when planning for
instruction in social studies and science.

For example, Bersh (2013) documented the use of thematic text sets on the
topic of immigration to support student knowledge of the topic and to enhance
social studies instruction. She further states, "The experience of [using thematic
text sets] provides an avenue through which their social awareness is enhanced
and leads to understanding difficult immigration-related problems such as rac-
ism, prejudice, and social injustice" (p. 50). Similarly, Folk and Palmer (2016) demonstrate the role of text sets when learning specialized content in science. The
thematic text set includes expository texts focused on the topic of optics and how
light and color affect the optic process. Lupo, Berry, Thacker, Sawyer, and Merritt (2019) expand on the process of creating text sets to develop what are called
"quad sets," as methods for developing background knowledge and for supporting reading comprehension. The quad component includes four distinct types of
texts:

- Visual or video texts
- Informational texts
- Accessible texts (nonfiction articles or young adult fiction)
- Targeted challenging texts

For example, to put this approach to rethinking text sets into practice, with
an emphasis on expository texts, we share an example related to the topic of
immigration.

- Visual or video texts: Video segments from Scholastic's *Immigration Stories of Yesterday and Today.*
- Informational texts, differentiated to meet students' developmental and instructional needs (e.g., *Coming to America: A Muslim Family's Story,* Wolf, 2003)
- Accessible texts, nonfiction articles, and young adult fiction:
  - *Mexican Migrant Workers in the 20th Century; https://www.commonlit.org/en/ texts/mexican-migrant-workers-in-the-20th-century*
  - *"They'll Kill Me If I'm Sent Back"* (Smith, 2019); *https://junior.scholastic.com/ issues/2018-19/012819/they-ll-kill-me-if-i-m-sent-back.html#970L*
  - *Other Words for Home* (Warga, 2019)
- Targeted challenging texts: *Coming to America: A Journey Home,* especially Chapter 2 (Tran & Hackman, 2019)

Like this example of rethinking how to develop thematic text sets to support and engage readers with expository texts suggests, developing text sets focused on providing multiple types and modes of expository text can be a powerful means of engaging students in learning and understanding specialized content, particularly in social studies and science.

In short, expository text is a unique genre that can be used to engage students in connecting with relevant and authentic topics. Teachers can use a variety of instructional approaches to connect teaching with expository texts. We emphasize the important role of expository texts in using children's literature to structure authentic and purposeful reading opportunities in classrooms.

PRACTICE

Expository text is an important genre that can be used to support vocabulary acquisition, connections with the real world, and student motivation. Understanding how to use this unique genre will ensure that students are developing the specific content knowledge and specialized knowledge needed to be successful.

ACTIVITY I. *Reflection Questions*

1. Review your classroom library. What is the breakdown of the types of books you have in your classroom? Do you have an equal number of the various types of expository texts and narrative texts?

2. As you review your read-alouds over the past week in your classroom, how many were read-alouds of expository texts? How did you decide on these topics? Did students have a say in selecting these topics?

ACTIVITY 2. *Planning a Project-Based Unit with Expository Text Sets*

Engaging students in real-life authentic tasks, in which expository texts are used as a catalyst for researching and finding answers to questions, and in which students write and discuss topics (the subject of the next chapter) is imperative in today's context.

- Check your state's social studies and science standards. We also suggest looking at the Next Generation Science Standards and the C3 Framework for Social Studies State Standards to understand the current guidance from national organizations.

- Invite students to brainstorm a list of interesting topics they would like to research.

- Help students structure their topics into researchable questions, using state and national social studies and science standards for guidance.

- Structure a 4-week unit in which students work in small groups to research their topic and produce an authentic product as a result of their research. For example, a sample outline might include:

  - *Week 1:* Posing questions and finding information through research in a variety of texts. Guide students by developing expository text sets using the approach outlined by Lupo and colleagues (2019). Select visual or video texts, informational texts, accessible texts (nonfiction articles or young adult fiction), or targeted challenging texts.
  - *Week 2:* Informal sharing with other groups to ask clarifying questions; additional research to verify information and find new information.
  - *Week 3:* Informal sharing with other groups to ask clarifying questions; begin planning how information can be shared to help other groups understand; additional research as needed.
  - *Week 4:* Informal sharing with other groups to share ideas about how to present information, create final projects, and plan presentations. Presentation ideas include developing a podcast about the topic, creating a brochure to share with the school and local community, or creating a book to share with others in the school. Work within your grade level to share your unit planning and your approach to showing your students how to conduct research using informational texts.

ACTIVITY 3. *Case Study*

Consider the following project that was developed as a result of our work in schools. Students in a third-grade classroom read expository texts on friction and force. After reading several expository texts on the topic, the students worked together to create a brochure that contained the information they acquired. The local parks and recreation department displayed the brochure at local park sites for visiting parents and community members to read. Foundational texts for the students' text set included:

- *Give It a Push or Pull* (Boothroyd, 2010)
- *Forces That Make Things Move* (Bradley, 2009)
- *Pushes and Pulls* (Coan, 2015)

ACTIVITY 4. *Using Children's Literature*

1. *The Moon Seems to Change* (Branley, 2015). Consider how informational texts can be used to invite students to engage with their local environment. *The Moon Seems to Change* (Branley, 2015) is an engaging book that features details and facts about the different phases of the moon. Using this text, students can engage in a monthlong reading and writing project to explore the different phases. Other texts that can be paired with this topic include *Next Time You See the Moon* (Morgan, 2014), *The Phases of the Moon* (Pendergast, 2015), and *The Moon Book* (Gibbons, 2019).

2. *A Women's Suffrage Time Capsule: Artifacts of the Movement for Voting Rights* (Stanborough, 2020). This powerful expository text captures all of the important events and people in the women's suffrage movement. Using this text, upper-grade teachers can have students work to create an informational handout on women's suffrage. Building on the quad text set approach, consider including other texts, such as video segments from the PBS series, *Not for Ourselves Alone* (Burns, 1999); firsthand accounts of the life of a pivotal figure in the movement, Elizabeth Cady Stanton, from the Library of Congress (Stanton, 1840); and *Elizabeth Cady Stanton as Revealed in Her Letters, Diary, and Reminiscences* (Stanton & Blatch, 1922).

CHAPTER 8

How Can We Use Writing and Discussing to Make Sense of Reading?

WHAT'S THE BIG IDEA?

We love children's and young adult books. In writing this this book, we've spent time sharing some of our personal favorite books from past and present. Our own passion to share reminded us that children's literature is not just about reading. Instead, children's books are really about communicating—we read to communicate with the authors and with each other and to understand ourselves. We read to communicate with others about texts.

Children's books give us something to talk and write about. They also provide the models for how to talk and write. The way in which writing and discussion connect with using children's literature is an integral part of developing classrooms where students are engaged in meaningful opportunities with the text. In this chapter, we focus on how discussion and writing can help students make sense of children's literature and how structured, meaningful opportunities in these areas can support purposeful reading opportunities in classrooms. We examine classroom situations where teachers engage in specific types of dialogue and practices to cultivate contexts where students engage meaningfully with the text.

WHAT ARE THE THEORIES?

The theory of social constructivism helps us understand how and why teachers use discussion and writing with their students to support opportunities where they can make sense of many kinds of text, including auditory, visual, and printed text. We highlight three critical elements of the social constructivist theory that are essential when thinking about how to use children's literature in the classroom.

Learning Is Situated

Learning is situated or contextualized in locally constructed settings where students' conversations, actions, and productions, such as writing and composing artifacts, inform their understandings of literacy. Although this observation may seem intuitive, as we mentioned earlier in Chapter 1, opportunities for students to engage in authentic literacy opportunities have been on the decline as a result of recent educational reforms (e.g., NCLB, 2001;U. S. Department of Education, 2009). Having a view of literacy learning that is specific and central to students' local surroundings, languages, and cultures is critical when conceptualizing how to put theory into practice. In this way, teaching becomes flexible and uses "the cultural knowledge, prior experiences, frames of reference, the performance styles of ethnically diverse students to make learning encounters more relevant to and effective for them" (Gay, 2000, p. 29). Teachers must consider students' backgrounds, lived experiences, and their specific teaching context as rich sites for exploration.

For example, consider how a fifth-grade teacher with whom we work uses the local environment as an opportunity to engage her students in literacy learning. In order to engage them in connecting with the need for reading expository texts for a real purpose, Ms. Daley structured an integrated science and literacy unit in a way that enabled her students to conduct research on their local environment, and through texts and resources to find solutions to an environmental issue right outside of their classroom. The school is located next to a creek, which in recent months became more and more polluted. Ms. Daley asked her students to photograph the creek over several days, noting the way the rain changed the water levels, and modeled for the class how to search city maps to find out where the creek started and traveled. She created a class research project focused on using a variety of texts and the local environment as sites for research and learning.

Students researched online the common pollutants in creeks and then put together a PowerPoint presentation for the school's parent–teacher organization with the aim of creating a schoolwide initiative about restoring the creek's banks and wildlife. As in other multifaceted learning opportunities, students engaged in a variety of authentic literacy tasks, from discussing the work collaboratively, to researching and reading to find solutions to their problem to creating an effective presentation that incorporated audio recordings and photographs of their findings. During these learning experiences, literacy learning became a social event that was specific to students' daily lives and the local environment that the community cared about and were invested in.

Learning Is Co-Constructed

Learning is co-constructed in that students make sense of what they are learning through collaborative processes. That is, students work together to make sense of what they are doing and thinking with other students and the teacher.

As in the above example, during the integrated science and literacy project, Ms. Daley encouraged group discussion and inquiry about students' questions, ideas, and thinking. In fact, the culminating research project for the unit on the local creek was a collaborative PowerPoint presentation that shared the collective knowledge acquired as a result of students' collective research. The class worked together to learn and read for a meaningful and authentic purpose. In this way, powerful opportunities for long-lasting learning experiences were developed as students and teachers co-constructed learning outcomes together and gained in-depth knowledge of what they read through social interactions (Morrow & Tracey, 2012). As you may recall from Chapter 5, the zone of proximal development (ZPD) and scaffolding are central to social constructivism (Vygotsky, 1978). The ZPD is the zone just beyond what a learner can accomplish alone, and scaffolding is the support that a teacher, for example, provides to help guide students within their ZPD.

In other words, Ms. Daley actively participated throughout this integrated unit modeling to students how to use their background knowledge about water levels, pollution, and the local creek and modeling to students how to extend their thinking. For example, for many of the students, measuring rainfall using a rainfall gauge was something they had not experienced before, and learning how to research public land documents to locate the creek's origin was also something new. Ms. Daley scaffolded students' learning in this concrete way but also through dialogue and interactions. She could be found listening to students' small-group discussions and asking them targeted questions to extend their thinking. In this way, learning was co-constructed and enhanced through interaction, and not an isolated activity (e.g., a worksheet) that students were left to complete on their own.

Language Is Foundational

Language plays a foundational role in social constructivist classrooms. Whether written or spoken, language is the means of communication that allows participants in the classroom to learn together. It is the way that teachers provide scaffolds for students in their ZPD. Language is also the way that meaning is negotiated. Previous researchers have suggested that language is necessary to create a community of students and adults who learn together, including giving students choices (Ivey & Johnston, 2015), increasing their motivation (Guthrie, 2008), and connecting with their out-of-school literacies (Alvermann, 2012; Dyson, 2003, 2020).

At the same time . . . children's conversations as they collaborate gives us a great deal of information about their literate development. The process also encourages children to talk, so we, and their peers learn more about them and their interests, and the vocabulary from those interests becomes distributed. The more we, and their peers, listen to them, the more seriously they take their own interests. (Johnston et al., 2020, p. 30)

Understanding that learning is situated and co-constructed and that language is foundational is vital when thinking about how to structure opportunities for writing and discussion in the classroom. Each of these three principles extends to how we use writing and discussion in the classroom to support and extend student thinking and learning around texts.

ACADEMIC CONVERSATIONS

For a few students, discussion seems to come easily, but most students (and sometimes teachers) have to learn how to have conversations that are meaningful and focused on content. We call these purposeful, connected conversations academic conversations. Academic conversations are the productive conversations that support the social construction of meaning, and, for our purposes, specifically meaning about texts. The CCSS call for these types of intentional (i.e., academic) conversations wherein students use core skills and practice using dialogue and language to convey their thinking and understanding. Accordingly, students must be able to "contribute accurate, relevant information; respond to and develop what others have said; make comparisons and contrasts; and analyze and synthesize a multitude of ideas in various domains" (NGA & CCSSO, 2010, p. 22).

When conceptualizing how to foster academic conversations, an intentional focus on the structures teachers scaffold to support them, in which students can contribute, respond, analyze, and synthesize, is useful. For example, sometimes the teacher initiates the academic conversation in a one-on-one conference with a single student using open-ended questions about the student's thoughts and reactions. In the following conversation between a fourth-grade teacher and a student about books the student is reading, you can see how the teacher elicited more information while listening to the student's initial response.

TEACHER: Can you tell me about some types of books you like to read?

STUDENT: I'm reading *The Warriors*, the second book in the series, but I really liked the series *Wings of Fire* too. It has so many things about the characters that I like. I really like fantasy books. Mythology is so fascinating. *Pegasus* is a mythology text, and the author Percy Jackson writes about that topic. I like mythology-type books because it's just so fascinating, the ideas of the different gods and the whole story comes to life and the monsters come to life.

TEACHER: You should read the *Fablehaven* series if you like series books like *Pegasus*. As you read these series books, tell me about the characters and any connections or differences you're finding. I'd like to hear what you think about the similarities and differences across these characters. Do you have any ideas so far?

STUDENT: In *Wings of Fire*, for example, I really like the way that they jump from different places—they jump across the character so that you see different perspectives, what the characters are thinking, and it just makes the plot so much more interesting. Although I think that the author should write other stories about some of the side characters like Kinkajou who don't have a full story in the book so we can know about their background.

TEACHER: I wonder if you want to start on something like that? What would you tell about Kinkajou? What do you already know, and what could you tell your readers?

Through the initial open-ended question, the teacher was able to pick up on the student's cues and scaffold the discussion even further. In this way, the teacher was adaptive and flexible in her approach and capitalized on her student's interests and responses. Effective teachers notice these opportunities for expanding on student inquiries and use them as a means to leverage meaningful academic conversations with their students. We discussed the role of adaptability in teaching (see Chapter 5), but want to highlight the adaptability required when scaffolding academic conversations with students.

> Excellent teachers demonstrated instructional adaptability (Spencer & Spencer, 1993), or an ability to adjust their instructional practices to meet individual student needs. For successful teachers, this flexibility appeared to be second-nature; they were able to sense and respond to diverse students and their changing needs (Allington & Johnston, 2002; Pressley et al., 2001). Wharton-McDonald and colleagues (1998) found that successful teachers were organized and prepared detailed lesson plans, but they did not follow them rigidly. Instead, they adapted plans as the need arose. (Vaughn et al., 2020, p. 300)

During the previous student–teacher exchange, the teacher listened, and during the discussion engaged the student in making connections across the texts and suggested a way to extend the student's thinking based on her ideas. The student shared that fantasy was her favorite genre and started to make several connections to other texts characters and reading preferences. The teacher extended the student's thinking and asked her to explore these connections more fully and also started to share additional recommendations of texts based on the student's interests. We recommend capitalizing on these moments when they arise during discussions with students so that you can help to model the essential skills of productive academic discussions (e.g., elaborating, synthesizing, comparing, and contrasting).

Much like the previous exchange suggests, productive academic conversations are different, depending on the task, the text, and the reader. As this student discussed book recommendations and ideas about the texts, the teacher's purpose and goal was to learn about her student's insights and preferences. We recommend engaging often in similar discussions about text preferences with students, but we also want to expand on other types of productive academic discussions that teachers should encourage.

Teachers think about ways to extend learning opportunities so that students engage in productive academic conversations with one another. Further, they make sure that students aren't only talking with them but are talking to each other. For example, when engaging first graders in discussions about making connections while reading the text *A Full Moon Is Rising* (Singer 2011), students share their emotions about their families, late-evening celebrations, and their ideas about being outside at night. Students sit in small groups and talk with one another as their teacher, Ms. Riley, listens as an observer. As students sit and share these connections, if their conversations veer off track or pause, Ms. Riley offers guiding questions like "I wonder what that would look like?" and "Tell and show each other and me more about what you are seeing."

One such way to support productive academic conversations is to use targeted questions like those asked by Ms. Riley, who was strategic in her use of questioning to elicit student responses when talking about texts with them. For example:

- "Tell your partner and me what you are thinking."
- "Tell your group something that you wonder about."
- "Talk with your partner. Can you tell us more about what you are noticing about the text/characters/events and be ready share with the whole group?"
- "In what ways does this information or story connect with your life, what else you've read, or what you see in the world?"

In this way, Ms. Riley is scaffolding her first graders' ideas and incorporating rich, layered questions to develop productive and engaged talk. Johnston and colleagues (2020) describe classrooms where children know that everyone in the class is considered a teacher, so that an atmosphere of learning from one another is clearly communicated, even to guests entering the room. In fact, this type of environment is an essential support for academic conversations.

As these targeted questions suggest, a kind of recursive process and dialoguing with students occur when understanding and engaging with texts. In other words, teachers share authority with students and create an atmosphere in which everyone in the class, teachers, and students alike, can participate and learn from one another. Purposeful academic conversations are marked by this kind of productive back-and-forth dialogue that allows participants as a group to explore a topic in depth. They are fostered through dialogic stances when the teacher shares learning opportunities with students and thereby embraces fully the three principles we've outlined about social constructivism. This talk lends itself to meaningful and engaged conversations in the classroom and supports students along their ZPD.

Zwiers and Crawford (2011) identified five core features, also called conversation moves, of productive, dialogic, back-and-forth academic conversations between students and between students and teachers (see Table 8.1 for examples):

1. *Elaborate and clarify:* Students provide more information about the topic when speaking. When listening, students ask for clarification when they are confused or unclear. They request additional information.
2. *Support ideas with examples and evidence:* Examples and evidence help explain ideas. Additionally, adding examples helps strengthen a claim or argument.
3. *Build on and/or challenge a partner's ideas:* Rather than simply posing new ideas, students need to learn to build on another's idea or sometimes counter the speaker's ideas with understanding and kindness.
4. *Paraphrase:* Paraphrasing shows that the participant is tracking and organizing the important components of the conversation. It serves as a way to evaluate understanding and verify that listeners and speakers are communicating clearly.
5. *Synthesize conversation points:* Synthesizing helps confirm the conversation's

TABLE 8.1. Examples of the Five Core Skills of Academic Conversations

Elaborate and clarify	STUDENT 1: Here is a specific detail about the book *My Name Is Gabriela.* Gabriel Mistral was from Chile and she loved to write and teach.
Support ideas	TEACHER: What evidence from the text can help to support what you are telling us?
Build on	STUDENT 2: Where in Chile was she from? What did she like to write? Did she go to school to learn to teach?
	STUDENT 1: Oh, she was from the Elqui Valley and could see the Andes Mountains from her window—see here on page 4. She would sit and teach her friends when she was younger and taught herself to read. She went and became a teacher.
Paraphrase	STUDENT 2: Okay, it sounds like Gabriel Mistral was always interested in writing and being a teacher since she was young. She grew up in Chile, near the Andes Mountains, and wrote many things.
Synthesize	TEACHER: You found important details from the text, such as where she was from, what she wanted to do, and what she eventually did.

purpose, verify understanding, and increase the likelihood of the conversation being remembered.

In fact, the CCSS call for students to have these types of academic conversations that use these core skills. Accordingly, students must be able to "contribute accurate, relevant information; respond to and develop what others have said; make comparisons and contrasts; and analyze and synthesize a multitude of ideas in various domains" (NGA & CCSSO, 2010, p. 22). Consider another example from a classroom in which we work. During a modeled lesson on how to listen and clarify when hearing students' summaries, two fifth graders share their understandings and targeted questions after hearing each other's summaries while reading expository texts.

> RAINA: The rains in Ethiopia greatly increase the flow of the water in the Nile River and make good farming land because of the dry land.
>
> MAISIE: Wait, I'm kinda confused, what about the farming land makes it good? Is it from what you said, the rains overflow into the dry land and then they become wet and rich after the rain? Is the Nile River in Egypt?
>
> RAINA: Yes, the Nile River is in Egypt, and you are right. The land is usually dry, but after the rainfall, the Nile River overflows and makes the land that used to be dry much wetter and ready for farming.

In this exchange, the students are practicing how to listen intently and pose questions when hearing something to clarify their understanding. Unfortunately, this kind of discussion is not always part of classroom conversations. Instead, many classroom conversations are dominated by the teacher—the teacher asks the questions, emphasizes correct answers, and evaluates responses, often referred to as I-R-F (initiation–response–feedback; Cazden, 2001). At other times, the teacher provides a model that can be valuable, but that excludes students from participating. Undoubtedly, teacher talk is an essential dimension and component of effective literacy instruction, but opportunities for students to discuss and engage in meaningful conversations about the text is absent.

In some cases, schools do provide time for student talk, but it seems as if students get off track or have very little to say, what Zwiers and Crawford (2011) call "interaction without depth" (p. 8). In Raina and Maisie's classroom, the teacher had heard many of these more superficial conversations. Prior to modeling the conversation that occurred with Raina and Maisie, the teacher inserted a mini-lesson on elaborating and clarifying after hearing students respond to summaries of their expository texts with comments such as, "that's cool," and "interesting." In order for students to have engaged and productive academic discussions about what they read, there must be a balance between teacher modeling and student talk.

In classrooms, instances of unproductive discourse led Zwiers and Crawford (2011) to observe that "rich conversations in school are rare" (p. 7). Still, the benefits of conversation in schools are many, including building academic language and vocabulary, strengthening communication skills, and valuing different perspectives with empathy (Johnston et al., 2020; van der Veen, van Kruistum, & Michaels, 2015; Zwiers & Crawford, 2011).

WRITING

Writing is an important tool that can be used to support students' thinking and understanding. It allows them to clarify their thinking for themselves, communicate with others, and in some cases extend the verbal work of discussion into a more reasoned and thoughtful form. Providing opportunities for students to write and respond to what they read is also an essential part of comprehension, including helping students create meaningful connections to the text.

We think about writing in two broad categories—informal and formal. Informal writing is writing that allows students to capture their thinking without worrying about being evaluated for grammar or spelling conventions or structure. Informal writing may be for personal use only, or it may be for an audience. Formal writing is writing that will be evaluated in some way, meaning it is always for an audience. Both categories of writing are important. As teachers, we want to offer our students opportunities for both types of writing so as to develop the habits of a writer (see Figure 8.1).

Informal writing opportunities with literature might include:

- Jotting a note to yourself about something you want to talk about with a partner.
- Annotating a question or connection in the text.
- Keeping a list of ideas to write about based on what you are currently reading.

In this class . . .

- We write every day.
- We use our ideas and convey them through drawings/writings/creations.
- We value what we write.
- We value what others write and have written.
- We write for ourselves and to share our ideas.

FIGURE 8.1. Habits of a writer.

- Reading response journals: Students can write about and respond to the texts they are reading and incorporate their ideas and preferences. The teacher can respond back to students about their ideas and thoughts.
- Sketch to stretch: Students can use this practice of drawing their thinking with quick sketches (Short, Harste, & Burke, 1996) to show they understand what they are reading as it pertains to a variety of skills (main idea, connections to the text, visualization, etc.)
- Graffiti wall: Students compose a list of important words and ideas from the texts, then work collaboratively to create a graffiti wall.
- Quick writes: Students are encouraged to either write according to a teacher prompt or a "free" quick write, wherein they summarize their ideas or important responses from what they've read.
- Visual representations: This is a broad category encompassing a variety of visual representations from charts to diagrams to graphic maps about the texts.

Formal ways of writing are also important. Here we focus on two: What are some approaches to connecting literature and writing? Although there are many, we focus on (1) teaching the qualities of good writing (i.e., ideas, organization, voice, word choice, sentence fluency, and conventions) and (2) incorporating broader approaches and interpretations of writing to use with literature. In formal writing, we teach students ways to more effectively communicate. Books provide a natural model for showing students how other authors have used these writing traits. A popular curricular scaffold for teaching writing is the 6 Traits, including ideas, organization, voice, word choice, sentence fluency, and conventions (Paquette, 2007). There are certainly other approaches to teaching writing, but regardless of the specific approach, books are preferable. By teaching writing with books, we also help broaden readers' experiences from reading to understand to reading like a writer (Ray, 1999).

CONNECTING LITERATURE WITH TRAITS OF WRITING

Picture books provide a natural avenue for engaging students in writing about the text. The six qualities of effective writing (i.e., ideas, organization, voice, word choice, sentence fluency, and conventions) provide a scaffold for students to use in their writing about literature (Spandel, 2005). Teachers can use these traits while organizing students' writing activities. For example, while reading *Eating the Alphabet: Fruits and Vegetables from A to Z* (Ehlert, 1989), students illustrated their own letters of the alphabet and then worked in small groups to illustrate an additional letter for a class book that the students created. The illustrated book was used for read-alouds and for independent reading time in the classroom. Thus, students followed the ABC pattern, learning to put the letters in the correct order while writing and creating pictures for their specific letters. Using the 6 traits in working with picture books can be a purposeful way to connect literature and writing together. See Table 8.2 for other ideas for using the traits to support writing with literature.

In addition, chapter books can also be used to teach the traits and engage students in meaningful literature- and writing-related activities (see Table 8.3).

In understanding that language and dialogue open up spaces for students when talking and when reading texts, there are several ways to engage students that emphasize the connections to reading, discussing, and writing. Here we focus on how multimodality opens spaces for students' approaches to texts that take into account their interests and life experiences in ways that extend beyond paper and pencil.

TABLE 8.2. Characteristics of Writing in Picture Books

Characteristics of writing	Picture books
Ideas: the main, overall message	*Enemy Pie* (Munson, 2000)
Organization: how the text is organized/structured	*Cloudy with a Chance of Meatballs* (Barrett & Barrett, 1982)
Voice: the author's voice or tone of the piece	*After the Fall* (Santat, 2017)
Word choice: the language and vocabulary used in the text	*Halloween Hoots and Howls* (Horton, 1999)
Sentence fluency: how the text reads or flows	*Take Me Out of the Bathtub* (Katz, 2001)
Conventions: grammar nuts and bolts	*Punctuation Takes a Vacation* (Pulver, 2003)
Presentation: how the text is displayed or shared	*Snowflake Bentley* (Martin, 2009)

TABLE 8.3. Characteristics of Writing in Chapter Books

Characteristics of writing	Chapter books
Ideas: the main, overall message	*The Magic Finger* (Dahl, 2009)
Organization: how the text is organized/structured	*The Wringer* (Spinelli, 1997).
Voice: the author's voice or tone of the piece	*Flora & Ulysses* (DiCamillo, 2016)
Word choice: the language and vocabulary used in the text	*Brown Girl Dreaming* (Woodsen, 2016)
Sentence fluency: how the text reads or flows	*Love That Dog* (Creech, 2001)
Conventions: grammar nuts and bolts	*The War That Saved My Life* (Bradley, 2016)
Presentation: how the text is displayed or shared	*Amelia's Notebook* (Moss, 1995)

PRACTICAL CONSIDERATIONS:
HOW CAN YOU INCORPORATE MULTIMODAL APPROACHES
TO WRITING AND DISCUSSION?

All of these approaches emphasize the ways in which students compose their reactions, thoughts, and responses to texts. The International Literacy Association (ILA) recently expanded its view of literacy from reading, writing, speaking, and listening to include composing and viewing. The ILA's recent emphasis on the expanded view of literacy supports these multimodal approaches. As teachers, we know many of our students spend much time interacting with screens. They speak to virtual assistants or message others in games. They talk about YouTube videos and create their own videos using their phones. Rather than distancing ourselves from these approaches, we recognize how the thinking processes involved mirror what we ask students to do in more traditional reading and writing. For example, talking about a video requires the same kinds of sequencing and summarizing, as well as listening, that talking about a book requires. Consider a recent exchange we had with a sixth grader about Minecraft.

MARGARET: Tell me what's going on in your game now.

MARCUS: Before I make a tool like a shovel, I first have to find the resources—like wood for the handle and a rock or some other kind of metal for the shovel part. And I would need a craft table to make the shovel.

MARGARET: Where would you get a craft table?

MARCUS: There's no store or anything, I have to go out, find a tree, and chop it down (that's assuming I already have a tool to do that; if not, I'd have to create that too).

In this way, Marcus was involved in not only thinking about where his person in the game was going, but also planning the specific steps needed to create tools and to find the resources to make the next move in the game. These types of decisions are just as sophisticated as interpreting a text. In addition to games like Minecraft, creating PowerPoints, composing multimodal artifacts with images, audio, videos, and the like, requires the same thoughtfulness that writing a story includes, with attention to the audience.

Initially, we were hesitant to think about incorporating multimodal methods into our own classrooms—we like the feel of a physical book, for example. But after a period of seeing the excitement students have when they are creating, composing, or using a variety of modes to share their ideas and thinking, well, it wasn't hard then to embrace multimodality in our approach to teaching. In fact, like other scholars, we realized that multimodality opened new possibilities and allowed us to think about all the ways that students respond to information and created and shared ideas. Like Whitin (2009), we've come to believe that "incorporating multimodal response strategies into everyday literacy instruction builds comprehension and literary interpretation while giving learners purposeful experience in using these modalities" (p. 408).

We know that students' responses to what they read, hear, or learn can be conveyed in multiple ways. Students can create sketches, collages, audio recordings, and other representations about what they read to facilitate discussions about literature. Digital technologies allow for visual strategies to be integrated into literature discussions as well. We welcome the use of a variety of technologies that aid in students' understandings and interpretations of and responses to texts:

- *Book trailers.* Using PowerPoint, students create book trailers about an important piece of literature.
- *Bless this book.* Using Word, students insert images to create visual representations of books, favorite characters, plot details, and other literary elements.
- *Digital movies.* Using this technology, students extend their understandings about topics, characters, plots, or other literary elements in books.
- *Online story developing tools.* These tools help students extend or reenact stories in digital formats (e.g., Toontastic).
- *Infographics.* Students can create their own infographic using *https://piktochart.com* to summarize textual information from informational texts.
- *Comics.* Students can create comic book panels using digital tools, such as *www.storyboardthat.com* or *https://piktochart.com,* to illustrate part of a story or compose their own story.
- *Coding.* Students create simple code using *https://code.org* to illustrate a scene from a book.

Ultimately, we take our cues from the students and their families. We learn daily from our students about new technologies that can be used to share information. For example, we learn about what students already use or what they want to use at home. We encourage them to think deeply about what they want to communicate and how they want to go about it. We also try to help them overcome their possible fears or hesitance about trying new methods and platforms. Moodley and Aronstam (2016, p. 2) summarize the importance of multimodality in classrooms today:

Techniques of sound, image and colour continue to have enduring effects on the form and function of reading as digital modes which offer different and unique ways of communicating the meaning of a message. Teachers have a responsibility to incorporate digital technologies into their literacy programmes to prepare learners by means of new modes of reading and writing that are prevalent in their world; not just limiting them to using traditional paper readers and big books (Javorsky & Trainin, 2014, p. 607).

In practice, we use three primary approaches to using multimodality in writing about and responding to literature that involve the following modes of instruction:

- Composing: Students can individually or collaboratively use a variety of tools to convey meaning about what they read.
- Orienting the tasks on the means of communicating, and inviting students to compose for a variety of purposes.
- Encouraging metacognition, or having students think about their thinking. Ask students about what they are composing and about the method they chose and encourage them to think deeply about why they are using a particular tool to convey the messages they want.

For example, consider a recent observation between a third-grade student and her teacher. The teacher read *The Orange Shoes* (Noble, 2007), a story about a girl who had a bright outlook on life but did not have any shoes or much money. The book describes the importance of staying true to who you are. After the read-aloud, the teacher modeled to students about how to create an All About Me presentation, using Flipgrid to show the things that were important to them. During the exchange, the teacher described a variety of ways the students could choose to display their information. During the planning phase, she met with students in small groups and individually to ask about their composing process.

TEACHER: Dahlia, tell me what are you going to do for your All About Me presentation. What tools are you going to use, and why?

DAHLIA: I really like horses, so I am going to use this picture of me on my grandpa's horse, Casper, to show. I think I'm going to add me talking, because I can tell about the time I was on Casper and we ran into a skunk.

In this exchange, Dahlia shared a specific rationale as to why she selected her image and tools for the audio recording of her story. The teacher conferred with the student to understand her thinking process. By doing so, the teacher could then scaffold Dahlia if any questions evolved during this stage of the writing process. Multiple modes of technology and materials such as photographs, painting tools, or paper and pencil can provide a way for students to think, compose, and respond to what they read.

In classrooms where teachers use children's literature purposefully, students are co-constructors of their knowledge, learning experiences, and activities. Social constructivism emphasizes the ways in which teachers can involve students in discussing, reading, and writing about literature. Students can use a variety of modes to capture and display their thinking.

PRACTICE

Writing and discussion are an integral part of purposeful reading opportunities. Students can engage in authentic discussions about what they read and participate in meaningful writing tasks that challenge and extend their thinking. Multimodality just involves a variety of modes you can use to support students' learning and understanding about what they read.

ACTIVITY 1. *Reflection Questions*

1. When you review your teaching practices, what are the opportunities for students to engage in relevant discussions about and meaningfully with texts and with one another?

2. What current activities or projects do you use to incorporate reading and writing with children's literature? How do you use technology and multiple modes (i.e., painting, collages, audio recordings, or photography) to engage your students? Why do you use the specific modes that you do, and are there ways to incorporate other modes as well?

3. Create your own Beliefs about Writing list that you can share with your students. Have them complete their own Beliefs about Writing. Talk together about your shared beliefs and develop Classroom Beliefs about Writing.

   Questions to consider when writing your own Beliefs about Writing:

   a. What do you think is important when it comes to writing? I think that _____ is important when it comes to writing because _____.
   b. What types of writing do you value? Why?
   c. What do you believe should motivate students when it comes to writing? Why?

   Questions to consider when asking your students to create their Beliefs about Writing:

   a. What do you think is important when it comes to writing? I think that _____ is important when it comes to writing.
   b. What types of writing do you value? Why?
   c. What do you believe will make you want to write? Why?

   Questions to consider when creating Classroom Beliefs about Writing:

   a. What do we value when it comes to writing?
   b. What types of writing are valued in this classroom?
   c. What do we believe will encourage us to want to write in this classroom?

ACTIVITY 2. *Developing a Sense-Making Approach*

As students read the text *El Deafo* (Bell, 2014), they were asked to make connections with the main character about their own lives, in and out of school. Students were asked to first sketch their ideas, then share them with a partner and find others who had similar or different experiences. Then the teacher asked the students to work collaboratively to share their group's ideas. Students were encouraged to write, draw, or use images online to share their experiences. In doing so, they were able to make sense of the character's experience with their own lives. These kinds of opportunities in which students can unpack and examine stories can facilitate a variety of academic and affective skills.

ACTIVITY 3. *Case Study*

Consider the following projects that were developed as a result of our work in schools.

Lu had come to the United States from China 4 months ago. In that time, she noticed how popular the books in the *Diary of a Wimpy Kid* (Kinney, 2007) series were. She began reading these books during independent reading and then taking them home. When asked to select a book project, she chose to create her own comic using StoryboardThat and imagine a new adventure for the main character, Greg Heffley. In talking with her about why she made these choices, she said that she enjoyed the books so much that she wanted to keep the stories going. Using comics helped her communicate without knowing all of the English words for everything she wanted to say because she could convey meaning through pictures, and others could understand what was happening.

Similarly, Ethan was a very reluctant middle school reader. Although he could read with comprehension, he didn't like to read and looked for ways to avoid reading if possible. Dixie, his teacher, had just used the *Who Would Win?* (Pallotta, n.d.) series to model how to write using multiple text features, such as charts, diagrams, and maps, to make informational text more understandable. Although the books were well below what some would have labeled his reading level, Ethan's imagination was fueled by them. When given the option to choose a book project to showcase what he had been reading, he opted to use a coding website to create a version of one text depicting the battle scene. When talking with him about his choices, he answered, "I don't know why I'm working this hard!" For one of the first times, he was completely engaged in a school task that included reading and writing.

ACTIVITY 4. *Using Children's Literature*

For this activity, create your own working list of at least two picture books or chapter books and accompanying traits.

- Ideas
- Organization
- Voice
- Word choice
- Sentence fluency
- Conventions

Building from the working list, what are one or two authentic activities you could do? Think about a variety of modes you might incorporate into these activities. What and why did you choose these specific modes?

Consider how the following books can be used to incorporate a multimodal approach to responding to books:

1. *Four Feet, Two Sandals* (Williams & Mohammed, 2007). In this text, two girls in a refugee camp become friends as they find a pair of sandals. They decide to share the pair of sandals and become friends in the process. Students can use the theme of friendship in the story to interview a classmate about his or her life, and then switch and be interviewed by their peers. Students can create posters, pulling out important quotes from the interview, and working collaboratively to make posters of their classmates.

2. *Bob* (Mass & Stead, 2018). A fantasy story about a girl who leaves a mysterious creature in her grandmother's house. Students could create their own visual representations using a medium of their choice (i.e., sculpture, painting, or digital image) to visualize the character, Bob, in the story. Students could then describe the character through class presentations.

3. *Echo* (Ryan, 2015). During a novel study of the book *Echo* by Pam Muñoz Ryan, which is a story about interconnected characters and a harmonica, students could respond to one another on the classroom blog, posting their predictions about what they think will happen next in the story and why. The class could read these predictions before the novel study discussion to gauge what the class's thinking is about the story.

CHAPTER 9

How Can We Encourage Reading Beyond the Classroom?

WHAT'S THE BIG IDEA?

Reading that students do in classroom settings is not enough to meet academic needs or to foster a love of reading. Most teachers and families would agree that we want students who lead literate lives beyond the classroom and to read for personal and professional reasons. If we want students to be able to lead literate lives both in and out of school, we must encourage them to read as much as possible.

WHAT ARE THE THEORIES?

In the previous chapter, we focused on instructional practices in the classroom. These practices are teacher driven and facilitated. If literacy is to occur beyond the classroom, we cannot expect families to follow the same instructional approach. Nor should we expect students to demonstrate traditional school literacies in their out-of-school lives. In other words, if we want students to value literacy, we need to expand our traditional views of literacy, learners, and social interactions that occur during school hours. If we are to encourage reading on a regular basis, we need to expand this view of what reading—indeed, of what all literacy—is and help students understand themselves as having valuable literate lives outside of the classroom (see Figure 9.1).

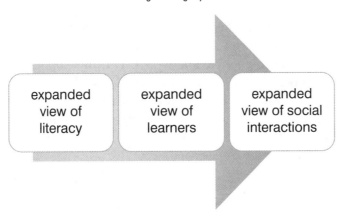

FIGURE 9.1. How can I encourage reading beyond the classroom?

An Expanded View of Literacy

The International Literacy Association's (2017) most recent standards expanded the definition of literacy to include viewing and visual representation along with reading, writing, speaking, and listening. Some might question how watching a YouTube video on making origami can be similar to reading a printed novel. While the actions themselves are different, comprehension of the text or video requires similar thinking processes, such as summarizing and monitoring understanding. When a reader reads a text or watches a video, he or she is also summarizing and monitoring understanding to gain meaning from the material. In another scenario, a person might synthesize information learned from a video, a painting, or a webpage using the same thinking processes as someone else reading multiple traditional texts. Similarly, composing a text, creating an infographic, developing a podcast, and writing a webpage all require attention to audience and literacy acts associated with comprehending, composing, and understanding. While participating in these activities, students can present a point of view, pose an alternative perspective, and engage in dialogue. The actual creation is based on creating a plan and writing and revising multiple drafts.

What we learn from the concept of emergent literacy also informs how we view the expansion of literacy. Before an emergent literacy view became prominent, many educators believed that students would read when they were ready. Referred to as "reading readiness," schools sometimes withheld formal instruction during the initial years of schooling (Crone & Whitehurst, 1999). Eventually, that thinking changed. Educators viewed the experiences that children encountered within the birth-to-5-year range as foundational for reading and literacy in general. For example, hearing oral stories affected students' vocabulary and sense of narrative. In turn, being read to influenced what words they might decode and how they comprehended text. Similarly, scribbles and formation of letterlike symbols were viewed not as nonsense, but as developmentally appropriate precursors to writing letters and words. This developmental approach to literacy helps us understand how students' experiences with literacy are cumulative and form a framework for future understanding.

Pahl and Roswell (2013) examined one component of emergent literacy: artifacts. Their research demonstrated how children used objects, such as dolls, to make meaning and describe events.

> Children's literacy experiences often connect to everyday objects and the meaning-making systems they offer . . . Much, if not all of the literacy practices as experienced by young children happen outside school contexts, and most happen in the home. It is important that early childhood literacy, therefore, adequately represents the experiences of children at home and acknowledges the diversity of home literacy practices. (p. 263)

Labeled *artifactual literacy*, the concept recognizes literacy as multimodal and situated within particular contexts. See Box 9.1 for an example of a classroom activity that uses artifactuality.

What does an expanded view of literacy have to do with encouraging reading—and all components of literacy—beyond the classroom? In a word, relevance. Recent surveys continue to find that leisure reading is at an all-time low. Making the connections between reading for authentic purposes is paramount. For example, consider the student who wants to be a mechanic. Arguing with the student about how much reading a mechanic does may be counterproductive. Motivational research emphasizes that readers are motivated by opportunities to pursue personally relevant answers to personally relevant questions. (Guthrie, 2008; Vaughn & Massey, 2019). For example, that same student who wants to be a mechanic might be highly motivated to read a manual on how to build a transmission or watch an online video of someone doing an axle repair. In essence, pursuing topics of personal relevance supports motivation to learn and a sense of self-efficacy or the belief that one can conduct and perform a task successfully (Bandura, 1977; Schunk, 1984, 1989; Zimmerman, 1989). Much like adults, students engage in a task when the likelihood of success is high and the perceived benefits outweigh the risks (Eccles & Wigfield, 2002).

The key to increasing students' practice of literacy is capitalizing on their goals and what they find relevant to achieving them. Many students are already actively involved in learning outside the classroom, whether it is at a boys' or girls' club, through extracurricular activities, or through their own searching online. Viewing this kind of learning as valid and relevant creates literacy opportunities for students to speak and write about what they are learning, as well as to listen to what others say about their own learning.

BOX 9.1. My Favorite Things

Guided by Pahl and Roswell's (2010) theory of artifactual literacy, pick two or three artifacts that have special meaning to you. Consider artifacts from different periods in your life. For example, perhaps it is a blanket from your childhood or a ticket stub from adolescence. In a small group, use the following protocol to talk about your objects:

ARTIFACT DISCUSSION PROTOCOL

Private thinking (5 minutes): Each individual in the group spends a few minutes writing down his or her responses to the following prompts.

- Why is this artifact important to you?
- When or where was this artifact meaningful to you?
- List three thoughts or feelings that you have when looking at this artifact.
- Is there a story connected with how you got the artifact or when you used the artifact?

Public group sharing (20 minutes—adjust as needed):

- Choose one person to begin.
- Give each person no more than 5 minutes to talk about their artifact. The person who is sharing can move sequentially through the private thinking prompts or choose one or two of the prompts to discuss in more detail.
- Each of the listeners may respond by asking a single question. Avoid using this time to share connections or similarities.

Public group discussion (10 minutes):

- As a group, share at least one thing you notice about artifacts.
- One person may be chosen to take notes.
- Conclude by creating a single group statement about the importance of artifacts that were shared in the group.

Public whole-group synthesis (10 minutes):

- Each group has an opportunity to share their group statement from the public group discussion.
- Allow time for follow-up questions or clarifications.

(continued)

Private reflection (5 minutes):

- Each person concludes by writing a thought or question on a note card about artifactual literacy.

In addition to considering artifacts that have special meaning in your life, think about ways that you can incorporate artifactual literacies into your classroom. This might include inviting students and/or their family members to bring in a special artifact. Instead of immediately asking them to write about their artifact, consider asking them to document their description of the artifact through photos and then asking them to capture their artifact through a variety of modes (i.e., speaking about it, acting it out, or drawing it).

Expanded Views of Learners

For much of the history of teaching, schools have focused on the cognitive and behavioral aspects of learners. Students are given particular designations that label them in the academic setting: if they are special education students, they are provided with individualized education plans (IEPs); or, if they are unmotivated students, they may be labeled "at risk" and are considered to be in need of additional support. In many schools, students are evaluated on how many words they read per minute. When talking with children, we have known several who tell us, "I read X words per minute," as if this is a part of their identity. Similarly, children describe themselves in terms of their reading level—"I'm a level H." Children start to view these labels as evidence that they are good readers or as evidence that they are poor readers. Not only do these labels define them, but they also become part of their academic identity.

Identity is not something that an individual *has*, but is an ongoing negotiation between the individual and the individual's larger context (Vadeboncoeur, Vellos, & Goessling, 2011). A person assumes multiple identities in relation to social and cultural communities and practices (Nasir & Cooks, 2009). For certain students, their academic identities are framed as deficient. Rather than focusing on the deficiencies of students, an expanded view of learners holds that deficiency is a social construct defined by the culture (Alvermann, 2001; Collins & Ferri, 2016; Goodley, 2007; Learned, 2016). Identities change on the basis of cultural contexts and communities of practice (Vadeboncoeur et al., 2011). Identity does not need to be something completely separated from learning, nor does it have to be a fixed entity. Rather, identity and learning can form reciprocal and ever-changing relationships, in that learning informs how one views their identity. Skills are continually developed within these communities (Nasir, 2002).

Letting students read and write what they want in the form that they want is critical to learners' identities. This approach is related to motivation theories, as discussed in Chapter 6. But allowing students some freedom with respect to what they read and write is also a way to let them explore and experiment with their own literate identities and demonstrate agency. Although we understand that students should and need to read and write for specific purposes that teachers outline, the fact is that most schools require the kind of reading and writing that students often dislike. However, if we want students to identify with literate practices in their day-to-day lives, then we need to allow them to explore the ways in which literacy exists outside of the classroom.

Expanded Views of Social Interaction

Digital technologies have exponentially expanded the possibilities for social interactions. Gallagher and Kittle (2018) described how their two high school classrooms collaborated around texts using video conferencing. In writing this book, we first wrote individually, then came together to write virtually in real time. The use of digital technology as a tool with which to collaborate around literacy is necessary for many students and adults alike. Hartman, Morsink, and Zheng (2010) noted that the interaction around a text can be nearly infinite—that is, multiple authors can contribute to Wikipedia, for example, even as multiple readers are all reading the same submissions.

Interaction doesn't only have to be something we can observe between people. It can occur between the characters and the text, as when the characters in a novel become real to the reader's experience. "Readers simulate the social experience by taking up perspectives of characters in the story and dealing with the conflicts they encounter" (Ivey, 2014, p. 167).

Why does an expanded view of social interaction matter to reading beyond the classroom? It is again a matter of relevance. Students want opportunities to interact around a text. Failing to consider students as social agents may limit their understanding and motivation to read (Ivey & Johnston, 2013, 2015). Interacting with peers around texts can increase students' abilities to make sense of the text (Santori, 2008), support their interest (Aukerman, 2013), help them navigate personal challenges (Ivey & Johnston, 2015), and encourage their sense of agency (Holland, Lachicotte, Skinner, & Cain, 1998; Ivey & Johnston, 2015). By agency, we mean that students have opportunities to make choices and decisions and to use what they know to transform their environment (Vaughn, 2014, 2018).

> The notion of student agency aligns with many tenets of teaching and learning . . . [Students] are increasingly capable of exercisving agency through such means as selecting a subtopic to study, choosing a book to read, determining how to execute a project in class, engaging with peers, or harnessing their

personal interests to elements of the curriculum. Indeed, providing space for students to recognize and cultivate their own agency is consistent with a developmentally responsive teaching and learning environment. (Wall, Massey, & Vaughn, 2018)

Yet one caution from the research is that we do not satisfy students' need for social interaction by simply putting them into groups. Instead, we need to scaffold opportunities when they can also form their own social interactions. For some students, that interaction may occur with a valued family member, as when a student describes a book to her grandmother, for example (Massey et al., 2017). For others, the interaction may take the form of participation in a fan group or online forum. Other students will form their own peer group organically based on who is reading the same text they are (Ivey & Johnston, 2015).

PRACTICAL CONSIDERATIONS

How Do You Invite Students into the Decision-Making Process?

Even with good intentions, creating requirements for specific literacy practices outside the classroom frequently backfires. Students may comply with requirements to read and keep a reading log at home, but their compliance rarely results in the kinds of engaged reading and learning that we hope to support.

We have begun to frame our discussions about encouraging literacy beyond the classroom as "opportunities and invitations" instead of requirements. That is, we offer students as many occasions as possible to try and expand their literacy leaning. We look at books that received awards by kids (see Appendix G: Children's and Teen Choice Book Awards). We ask students to choose their own award-winning books from the books they've read. Award names can be humorous, such as "Best book to read under the covers at night," or serious.

We try to spend more time talking about books. When adults read books, they frequently find a setting where they can discuss the books, such as a book club or over coffee with a friend. We want to mirror adult literate behavior with our students. We ask students to choose a book that they've read outside of class and have a conversation about it over lunch in the classroom. We ask students to recommend books that we do not have in our classroom libraries and leave us a note about why they think we should read the book. One of our recent invitations was based on a book we read by Pamela Paul (2017) called *My Life with Bob.* Paul kept a list of all the books that she's read since she was a junior in high school—hence the "Bob" in the title, which stands for "Book of Books." She describes how she keeps the lists (of titles and authors), why she includes books she hasn't finished, and most important, what she's learned about her own reading habits, as well as about herself from her book of books. We were so inspired that we began keeping our own book of books, modifying it according to our own preferences.

We began offering this suggestion to students and continuing to talk about our lives as readers outside of the classroom. Students may not accept our first invitation or even our fifth or sixth, but we keep inviting them as a way to show our commitment to them and our stance toward literacy.

Summer Access

Allington and McGill-Franzen have written extensively about summer reading loss. In their book *Summer Reading: Closing the Rich/Poor Reading Achievement Gap* (Allington & McGill-Franzen, 2018), they note that a major contributing factor to the rich–poor reading achievement gap is the amount of voluntary reading done during the summer. In the research conducted by these authors and others, providing access to books has been critical to helping students choose to read during this time, with the caveat that students need to have access to books that they can and want to read. Allington et al. (2010) met these demands when they allowed students to self-select titles from a school book fair and then read from the books for 1 or 2 minutes to verify if they were a good fit for them. In making their selections, the research team noted that the lowest readers struggled to choose books that they could read. Nevertheless, the researchers and teachers sent students' self-selected books home with students over the summer. Not only did the students read the selected books, but they also demonstrated increased comprehension achievement.

We understand that providing access for students can be a challenging task without simple solutions. It is also a very contextualized challenge that is best addressed by educators within their local community. As in the Allington et al. (2010) study, grants can be useful for purchasing books. Collaborating with local libraries is another way to connect kids and books. We know of one individual who started placing books in doctor's offices and attaching a short explanation for how to enjoy the book. High school students can choose book drives as part of their service projects, and the books that are collected can then be placed in Little Free Libraries within the community. The bottom line is that if we really want to encourage reading beyond the classroom, we need to find creative ways to help students and their families access texts during the summer and year-round.

Finding Personal Goals

Kids are amazing. Elementary school children choose to ask friends and family for donations to local animal shelters and homeless shelters instead of birthday gifts. Tweens come up with apps that are downloaded by millions. Teens patent inventions and create start-up companies to save the planet. Young people organize and demonstrate against gun violence. These youth have found a cause that they are passionate about because it is relevant to them.

If we want to encourage students to lead literate lives, we should help them explore areas that are relevant to them. Once they have identified what is important, we can help them find ways to spread their messages. When kids ask for donations, advertise an idea, or organize a movement, they need a way to get the word out, often through advertising, letters, blogs, websites, and more. In that way, literacy becomes one tool they use to accomplish their goals.

Some students seem to zero in on projects that are personally relevant almost immediately, while others struggle to find a project that they are passionate about. And while helping students find personal relevance has typically been relegated to time outside of school, what if they began exploring personally relevant topics during class time? As we discussed in Chapter 7, Google allows its engineers to devote up to 20% of their workday on projects of their own choosing. Google is one of many companies that has instituted this innovative practice in the belief that by allowing employees to work on something that interests them, productivity will go up.

Some schools have adapted the idea of personally relevant topics into "Genius hour projects." Students are given a specified time each week to explore a topic of their choice. They also choose how they will share what they learn. Over time, they may choose to switch topics or to delve deeper into the same topic. The teacher facilitates learning by asking questions, connecting students with resources, and offering ideas about how to communicate with others. By providing the time in class to pursue personally relevant topics, students learn what they're interested in, how to find out more about it, and how to network with others interested in the same ideas. This passion frequently fires an interest to keep going outside the confines of school time.

In this chapter, we have considered why reading in class is not enough to truly help students become readers. We need students to read beyond the classroom. In order to support students who love to read, we need to do more than simply assigning outside reading. Instead, we need to expand our views of literacy, of learners, and of social interaction. We need to help students see reading as a tool for learning in order to meet their own personal goals.

PRACTICE

ACTIVITY 1. *Questions for Reflection*

1. How does an expanded view of literacy, of learning, and of social interaction support reading beyond the classroom? What other ways of expanding our views of literacy, learning, and social interaction could be added?

2. What ways have you observed students leading literate lives outside of class? What seems to support these actions?

ACTIVITY 2. *Literate Lives*

Can a teacher encourage reading and writing if she is not reading and writing herself? In *Igniting a Passion for Reading* (2009), Steven Layne used the title "My Modeling Career" to emphasize the importance of showing students his own literate life by sharing what he was reading with them. In *180 Days* (2018), Kelly Gallagher and Penny Kittle describe their own writer's notebooks, including how and when they write outside of school and their challenges with writing. They include excerpts from their writing in the book. In *Reading with Meaning* (2013), Debbie Miller includes a mini-lesson in which she shares what she's reading with her primary students. The common theme? Teachers who want to encourage students to lead literate lives model how they incorporate literacy into their own lives.

We acknowledge the challenge of leading literate lives when the work of teaching places numerous requirements on a teacher's time and energy. At the same time, we believe it borders on hypocrisy to hope that students will read and write beyond the classroom when we as their models are unable to find space to do so as well.

We recommend creating a notebook, either virtual or physical, wherein you track the following elements. Treat the notebook as your first step toward including more literacy in your personal life!

1. Catalogue your own reading and writing for one week or more. What types of reading and writing or composing do you do? For what purposes do you read and write?

2. Set a personal goal for including reading and writing or composing in your week: start small and be realistic. Read one new article that interests you. Listen to an audiobook during your commute. Write one poem. Use an audio note on your phone to record favorite words and phrases to use in future writing. Create a blog.

3. During week two, set a separate goal. If more reading was your first goal, try to include more writing or composing in your second week.

4. Begin creating a list of topics to read and write about. One of the biggest barriers to continued reading and writing is the uncertainty of what to read or write about next. Try to include a variety of types of reading and writing that you wouldn't normally choose. If reading graphic novels doesn't usually appeal to you, get a recommendation from your students for a graphic novel they enjoyed and read it. The goal is to expand your repertoire of literate activities over time.

5. Share your notebook with your students. Don't be afraid to discuss your challenges.

Keep in mind two cautions. First, expect this project to feel like work if you are not someone who reads or writes during the school year. At some point, accomplishing your personal goals will feel like work and require discipline, whether it's training for a 5K race, learning a new language, or mastering a new piece of music. The practice it takes to reach a goal is not always fun. Waiting for something to be enjoyable is a sure way to make sure that it is never accomplished.

Second, don't turn your own literacy activities notebook into an assignment for students. This is your own work. It can certainly serve as an invitation or a model, but it is ultimately about your own personal growth. Turning it into a student assignment will create a sense that it is just another task you need to accomplish for your teaching life.

ACTIVITY 3. *Case Study*

Unfortunately, many studies have observed that students' willingness and motivation to read in their free time decline as they enter the intermediate grades and middle school. For that reason, this case study focuses on middle school readers. The following notes were taken from interviews with four students who were identified by the school as needing additional reading support.

1. Jake said that he liked books better than video games or television. He told his tutor that he believed the books he read in school provided information to get good grades. During the summer, he said he read maybe 10 minutes a week.

2. Ayaan had been in the United States for 3 years. According to school records, she was reading three levels below her grade. She sometimes read books that her sister recommended, such as romance novels. She described reading at home because "Sometimes I can forget everything around me. It helps me when I'm sad or angry. I read so I have something to do." She could not describe a time when a teacher had recommended a book to her.

3. Kyle liked to ask his school librarian what to read. He said that he liked to stop and talk about what he was reading. When asked what kind of reader he was, he said, "I wasn't a good reader last year because I read slower, but now I'm a good reader because I can read really fast." Kyle had extensive background knowledge about a variety of subjects. He was used to looking up information online when he encountered something he didn't know. When asked if he thought the information online was always reliable, he said, "I find it on Google; it must be true."

4. Jessie was a sixth grader with extensive knowledge of the Punic Wars. She was very interested in reading the texts that she chose. She described losing

track of time when she was learning about World War I during school. She went home and read more about World War I and played video games connected to World War I. She explained that sometimes she feels really bored when teachers tell her what to read.

Consider:
- What do you notice about these students' literate practices in the classroom?
- How would you compare these students' literate practices outside of school to their experiences in class?
- How would you invite these students to continue their literacy practices outside of school?

ACTIVITY 4. *Children's Literature*

We spend a lot of time recommending books to kids. For this activity, we encourage you to get the recommendations of students you know. Be sure to ask them why they like the books or why they think you should read them.

To get you started, here are some recommendations we have received from students:

- *The One and Only Ivan* (Applegate, 2012): because it's cool to think about how a gorilla would sound, and it's based on a true story.
- *Captain Underpants* (Pilkey, 1997): because it's funny.
- *The Crossover* (Alexander, 2014): because it is a good story, it's short, and it's cool
- *Don't Let the Pigeon* (Willems, series): because pigeon is always doing crazy things.
- *Elephant and Piggie* (Willems, series): because Piggie is nice.

CHAPTER 10

How Do We Put It All Together?

We began this book by emphasizing how children's literature can support students as they become agentic readers who read books with understanding and for enjoyment. In order to support readers in this quest, we focused on exploring and expanding our knowledge of teaching, of students, and of books in an effort to create purposeful reading opportunities.

WHAT'S THE BIG IDEA?

In order to connect with the theories and practices presented in this book, it is essential to remember what our mentor always says to us, "Keep the main thing, the main thing." In that spirit, we want to emphasize the following "big idea": *To construct purposeful reading opportunities, students must feel agency and engage meaningfully and authentically with texts.* We must keep in mind that students need to have agency. By agency, we mean that students must be supported in their:

- *Intentions.* To support developing students who have intentions, we must support opportunities for them to understand that reading is free—that students can read anything of interest. (The same is true of writing.) Thus, developing an awareness of and embedding practices to support authentic reading opportunities centered on students' linguistic, cultural, and life experiences and backgrounds are essential.

- *Knowledge.* At the core of what we do when we use children's literature in our practice is to cultivate agentic readers who have knowledge and skills, so that they can read and pursue their interests and obtain knowledge in the process.

This means that we co-construct learning opportunities that are flexible and that allow students to work alongside us to gain knowledge and skills.

• *Opportunities to transform.* In cultivating authentic and purposeful reading opportunities, we want to create readers who possess intentions and knowledge and who can use reading as a tool to transform their environment. We want our students to understand that, at its core, reading is a tool to be used for a variety of purposes and functions.

Keeping this "big idea" in mind, we invite you to connect the ideas from across these chapters and develop your own action plan or approach to using children's literature purposefully in the classroom. You can focus on incorporating your vision, beliefs, and knowledge.

WHAT ARE THE THEORIES?

Theories are our systems of beliefs. We all have theories about teaching, and we have considered many theories in this book. We have introduced several theories that inform how we use children's literature to teach students. In the following sections, we review the main ideas about the theories that have been discussed.

Theories about Teaching: Beliefs and Visions

Teaching purposefully requires developing a belief system that acknowledges that reading is an open invitation to students, giving them purposeful opportunities in the classroom to read all types of books and materials. How do you structure purposeful opportunities for your students? What are your central beliefs about what these opportunities should look like in classrooms where students are agentic readers?

Understanding that students want choice in the types of texts they want to read is paramount. Classrooms where teachers structure purposeful reading opportunities have three essential features: (1) students select books that interest them, (2) students have access to a wide variety of reading materials and texts, and (3) students are invited into the decision-making process. In other words, students are essential and active participants in the process of structuring purposeful reading opportunities—from offering input about texts, to providing direction about what they need as readers to be successful, to describing the types of tasks they can do to convey their knowledge about texts and the multitude of reading opportunities in your classroom. To summarize, a core structure for developing purposeful reading opportunities in your classroom includes the TACKLE approach (*Time, Access, Consider, Keep, Listen,* and *Engage*). We outlined this structure in Chapter 2 and emphasized that your instruction methods, guided by your vision and beliefs, change over time.

One way to critically reflect on your instructional approach is to develop a vision for how to teach reading and to use children's literature in your classroom. Your vision can serve as a guide for how you wish to structure your classroom and the skills you want to develop in your students, as well as for your own learning trajectory. Beliefs, knowledge, and vision go hand in hand. As you reflect on what you have learned as a result and acquire new knowledge, your beliefs inform your vision for teaching. This process is recursive and changes as you acquire new knowledge and beliefs and have a variety of experiences. Your vision evolves as you evolve as a teacher.

Theories about Literacy: Expanding Views of Literacy

We discussed three central theories as they pertain to literature: text-focused literary theories, reader-response theories, and context-oriented theories. To summarize, text-focused literary theories rely on the text and the message it conveys. The roles and influence of the author, the wider context, and the reader are purposefully excluded—meaning resides in the text alone.

In contrast to text-focused theories, reader-response theories view meaning as something that develops as the reader interacts with the text. In this view, there are multiple meanings and considerations. Context-oriented theories constitute the third broad strand and encompass feminist literary theory, gender theory, and Marxist theory. In these varied theories, texts are considered to be connected to a larger context, such as politics, genre, gender, or nationality, and positionality. Which group of theories do you use and when? None of these theories is a "silver bullet"; rather think about what your students need, what the text offers, and what skills you are trying to support in your students when promoting literacy learning.

Literacy learning takes place on a broad spectrum. Understanding the various modes students can use to develop literacy, such as speaking, visual representation, and digital technologies, are essential when thinking about expanded views of literacy. Incorporating opportunities in which students can use a variety of modes when engaging with literacy in your classroom is essential. Continue to think about how they can practice synthesizing while viewing a video, a painting, or a webpage and while using the same thinking processes as someone else reading multiple traditional texts. Although we have chosen a variety of traditional texts as the main mode of teaching in this book, we continue to think about ways to apply this expanded view of literacy. Possible ideas include asking students to both listen and view, as well as to create podcasts, blogs, and/or videos to tell stories or express ideas. Think about the various ideas presented in Chapter 9 about how students can move beyond print in applying their comprehension skills.

Theories about Readers: Funds of Knowledge and Motivation

Students in today's classrooms possess valuable experiences, ideas, languages, and beliefs. Understanding and valuing the funds of knowledge (Moll et al., 1992) students have are essential components of structuring purposeful reading opportunities. Indeed, literature can serve as windows, mirrors, and sliding glass doors (Bishop, 2009), allowing students to see themselves and others, and can serve as a means of transforming their views and ideas. Incorporating multicultural materials wherein students see themselves, see others in a culturally responsive manner, and engage with texts that depict individuals doing amazing things is a central consideration and should be the standard by which you structure reading experiences in your classroom.

Students need a variety of opportunities to read diverse materials and texts. They should become familiar with authors from diverse backgrounds and experiences as well as with using reading as a tool to learn about their own lives. Remember that students are highly motivated to read texts of their choice about interests that are relevant to their lives. Providing opportunities for engagement with authentic and relevant literature is a central component of purposeful reading.

Theories about Texts and Tasks

Texts are an essential part of a purposeful reading approach. Students must have opportunities to read authentic texts and real stories rather than text excerpts. No student ever has been excited to read a worksheet. Just as providing authentic literature is essential, students must engage in meaningful and authentic tasks when discussing, reading, and writing about texts. The types of tasks we ask students to do in reading literature are not only important, but also mirror what we believe about reading. Is reading about sense making? Is it for enjoyment? Or, is it a combination of both? When structuring purposeful reading opportunities, we must think strategically about the types of tasks and texts. Encouraging students to read widely is also part of structuring a purposeful approach to reading and using children's literature. Although students may continually gravitate toward certain genres, we must also encourage and ask them to expand their reading preferences.

HOW DO YOU PUT THESE IDEAS INTO PRACTICE?

Revisit your vision statement and think about revising it after reflecting on your knowledge about texts, tasks, and readers, as well as about the additional theories (i.e., comprehension, motivation, and student agency) presented in Chapters 5 and 6. Create a vision-to-action chart (see Figure 10.1) of what targeted

Dimension of your vision	What instructional practices?	Why these instructional practices?	How will you know you are working toward this dimension of your vision?
What is your vision for reading?			
What is your vision for using children's literature?			
What is your vision for your students?			
What is your vision for yourself as a teacher?			
What is your vision for your classroom?			

FIGURE 10.1. Vision-to-action chart.

instructional practices you will structure in your classroom to support dimensions of your vision.

Reflecting on the main ideas of the theories presented in each chapter, how does your vision connect with the theories outlined? Reflect on incorporating a purposeful approach to your reading program. How will you set aside the time for students to read and give them access to authentic texts, consider students' perspectives and interests, listen to students, and engage students with reading?

Although there is no single way to put these ideas into practice, there are a few key teaching practices that are critical in supporting reading comprehension. These practices allow for a flexible, student-centered approach to using children's literature, and include the following:

- Adaptive teaching (flexibly applying instructional opportunities to what students need in the moment).
- Gradual release of responsibility (modeling to students and then "releasing" the responsibility to the students).
- Translanguaging (providing a space where students can make sense of what they read, using multiple languages).

Purposeful teachers embed these practices in foundational knowledge, including their knowledge of books, of students, and of teaching. In order to build an effective pedagogy for using children's literature, we need to know books—lots and lots of books—as well as other print and visual materials. We need to be readers, consumers, listeners, and networkers. We need to ask students what books they like and take their recommendations seriously. We also need to introduce them to new books. This task is ongoing. We cannot rely on our knowledge of the books we enjoyed as kids or what our previous class enjoyed.

At the absolute heart of our work are the students. We need to know more about the specific students in our class. We need to know their interests, strengths, challenges, and habits. We need to honor their choices. As students understand and enjoy texts, they learn to act in agentic ways. By incorporating student writing and discussions about texts, we help to ensure that they will be interested and engaged in what they are reading.

Consider how your classroom library and classroom are organized. Who has access to books? How are you incorporating expository text, for example, in your classroom? Ensure an engaged and inviting classroom by organizing your space so that all students have equal access to books and materials of their own choosing, regardless of what their reading level is. Ensuring that students have multiple opportunities to self-select materials based on their interests and passions is paramount.

Finally, we need to continue to expand our knowledge of teaching by attending workshops, reading books about teaching, and interviewing other teachers.

Ultimately, these activities are not just about teaching. They are about maintaining our stance toward continual learning.

1. **Read!** We make it our goal to regularly read a balanced diet of professional books and children's/young adult books.
2. **Talk.** We talk to as many students as possible. We ask our own children what they like and what their friends like. We use our time in classrooms to have conversations with kids. We talk with other teachers to learn what they are doing. We talk to librarians.
3. **Share.** We constantly try to share our thinking with others. This book began as our informal sharing of ideas. We confess that we started with more questions than answers. Sometimes we share in formal ways, such as at conferences. We have found that making our thinking public allows us to refine our thinking in ever-deepening ways.

In conclusion, we advocate for incorporating children's literature in your classroom and life. Now, go and read!

Books to Support Student Agency

Title	Suggested grade level	Summary
Sam and Dave Dig a Hole Barnett, M. (2014)	K–2	Two brothers embark on a journey to dig a hole. They demonstrate persistence and agency as they continue to dig until they find something spectacular.
Dreamers Morales, Y. (2018)	K–2	This book documents what immigrants may bring with them as they travel to their new home. Yuyi shares her experience with her son as they travel from Mexico to the United States.
A Splash of Red: The Life and Art of Horace Pippin Bryant, J. (2013)	3–5	This book documents Horace Pippin's journey as an artist from child to adult. The book offers an important portrait of how to overcome obstacles.
Fall in Line, Holden Vandever, D. W. (2017)	3–5	This story documents the experience of Holden, a young Navajo student, as he navigates boarding school. It teaches readers about resistance and about overcoming barriers.
Wonder Palacio, R. J. (2012)	3–5	This book is the story of how a boy who has facial differences that make school challenging overcomes bullying and other obstacles.
I Am Malala: The Story of a Girl Who Stood Up for Education and Was Shot by the Taliban Yousafzai, M., & Lamb, C. (2013)	6–8	This autobiography tells the story of Malala, who was shot after she was critical of the Taliban's rule in Pakistan. She survived and continues to work for the education of women worldwide.
Long Way Down Reynolds, J. (2019)	6–8	This book tells the story of a boy who plans to seek revenge for the murder of his brother. Told in free-verse poetry, the story covers just 60 seconds of time as the main character struggles with his decision.
March Lewis, J., Ayden, A., & Powell, N. (2013)	6–8	*March* is a trilogy of graphic novels that tell the story of John Lewis, the author, within the broader narrative of the Civil Rights movement.

Books to Talk about Visioning with Students

Title	Suggested grade level	Summary
Daniel Finds a Poem Archer, M. (2016)	K–3	Daniel has a vision of using the outdoors to create poetry.
The House That Lou Built Respicio, M. (2019)	K–3	Lou has an idea for building her own house. This text outlines her vision of having her own space and how she plans to create it.
The Vast Wonder of the World: Biologist Ernest Everett Just Mangal, M. (2018)	1–5	This text is a biography of Ernest Everett Just, who changed how the world looked at biology. He had a strong vision of viewing the world that shaped how he grew as a biologist.
My Beijing: Four Stories of Everyday Wonder Jun, N. (2018)	1–5	This book shows how a young girl with an unspecified physical disability navigates the world. She dreams of becoming a champion swimmer and holds on to this vision throughout the story.
Echo Muñoz Ryan, P. (2015)	6–8	This is a powerful story of multiple characters that explores how passions and stories shape who we are.
Rebound Alexander, K. (2018)	6–8	This prequel to *The Crossover* told in free verse explores the story of Chuck Bell. Initially, he is an unhappy boy who sees himself as a victim. Over time, he finds his goal, and this discovery changes the course of his life.
They Called Us Enemy Takei, G. (2019)	6–8	This graphic novel narrates George Takei's experiences as a boy in a Japanese internment camp and selected experiences from his adult life. Throughout the book, Takei casts a vision of kindness toward all people.

Books by Genre

The following are other anchor texts that show the conventions of genre. Remember that you can use all of these books with any of the three literary theories reviewed in Chapter 3.

Folk Literature/Folktales/Fairytales

Perez y Martina by Pura Belpre
The Dragon Slayer: Folktales from Latin America: A TOON Graphic by Jamie Hernandez
Cinderella's Dress by Shonna Slayton
Troy High by Shana Norris

Science Fiction

Fly Guy by Tedd Arnold
Eager by Helen Fox
Percy Jackson and the Olympians by Rick Riordan
The Giver by Lois Lowry

Biography/Autobiography

Balloons over Broadway by Melissa Sweet
I Dissent: Ruth Bader Ginsberg Makes Her Mark by Debbie Levy
Our Children Can Soar: A Celebration of Rosa, Barack, and the Pioneers of Change by Michelle Cook
Malala: My Story of Standing Up for Girls' Rights by Sarah J. Robbins
Tasting the Sky: A Palestinian Childhood by Ibtisam Barakat

Realistic Fiction

Ling & Ting: Not Exactly the Same by Grace Lin
Clara Lee and the Apple Pie Dream by Jenny Han

Reaching for the Sun by Tracie Vaughn Zimmer
The Hate U Give by Angie Thomas
Out of My Mind by Sharon Draper

Historical Fiction

Cats in Krasinski Square by Karen Hess
Chains is the first book in the Seeds of America Trilogy by Laurie Halse Anderson
Code Talker: A Novel about the Navajo Marines of World War Two by Joseph Bruchac
Freedom in Congo Square by Carole Boston Weatherford
Martin's Big Words by Doreen Rappaport

Graphic Novels

Jack and the Box by Art Speigelman
Zita & the Space Girl by Ben Hatke
Lunch Lady series by Jarrett J. Krosoczka
Illegal by Andrew Donkin and Eoin Colfer
New Kid by Jerry Craft

Poetry

Daniel Finds a Poem by Micha Archer
When Green Becomes Tomatoes by Julie Fogliano
Can I Touch Your Hair? Poems of Race, Mistakes, and Friendship by Irene Latham and
    Charles Waters
For Everyone by Jason Reynolds

Narrative Nonfiction

Giant Squid by Candace Fleming
Phineas Gage a Gruesome but True Story about Brain Science by John Fleischman
We Are Not Yet Equal: Understanding Our Racial Divide by Carol Anderson

Expository Nonfiction

Eye to Eye: How Animals See the World by Steve Jenkins
Robert Capa, Gerda Taro, and the Invention of Modern Photojournalism by Marc Aronson and
    Marina Budhos
Grand Theft Horse by Gregory Neri
Samurai Rising: The Epic Life of Minamoto Yoshitsune by Pamela S. Turner

Book Awards

Award	Description
American Indian Youth Literature Award	This award was established in 2006 and is given every other year to honor writing and illustrations by and about American Indians and Alaska Natives. Previous award winners include *Tales of the Mighty Code Talkers: Volume One* edited by Arigon Starr and *Shanyaak'utlaax: Salmon Boy*, published by Sealaska Heritage Institute.
American Book Award	The American Book Award was created to recognize exemplary literary achievement "from the entire spectrum of America's diverse literary community." There are no categories or nominees for this award.
Carter G. Woodsen Book Award	The National Council of Social Studies gives this award to distinguished social science books that depict ethnicity in the United States. This award is given to books at each of the primary, middle, and older grade levels. Past winners include *The Vast Wonder of the World: Biologist Ernest Everett Just* by Mélina Mangal; *America Border Culture Dreamer: The Young Immigrant Experience from A to Z* by Wendy Ewald; and *A Few Red Drops: The Chicago Race Riots of 1919* by Claire Hartfield.
Pura Belpré Award	The Pura Belpré Award honors a Latinx writer and illustrator whose work portrays and celebrates Latinx culture. The award is named after Pura Belpré, the first Latina librarian at the New York Public Library. Past winners include *The Poet X* by Elizabeth Acevedo and *Dreamers*, written and illustrated by Yuyi Morales.
Tomás Rivera Award	Tomás Rivera was an author and scholar whose life as part of a migrant family is told in the children's book, *Tomás and the Library Lady* written by Pat Mora. This award is given to authors and illustrators whose work honors and celebrates the Mexican American experience. Past winners include *They Call Me Guero* by David Bowles and *I Am Not Your Perfect Mexican Daughter* by Erika Sanchez.

Award	Description
Notable Social Studies Trade Books, bibliography	This bibliography of multiple books is sponsored by the National Council of Social Studies. Books are chosen on the basis of their representation of diverse groups and for their emphasis on human relations. Books are matched to the 10 thematic strands of the National Council of Social Studies Curricular standards. Books that have appeared on the list include *John Ronald's Dragons: The Story of J. R. R. Tolkien* by Caroline McAlister; *John Deere, That's Who!* by Tracy Nelson Maurer; and *Frederick Douglass: The Lion Who Wrote History* by Walter Dean Myers.
Asian/Pacific American Literature Award	This award is given to books that honor Asian/Pacific American culture and heritage. There are five categories of awards, including two for adults, as well as awards for young adult, children's, and picture books. Winners include *Darius the Great Is Not Okay* by Adib Khorram; *Front Desk* by Kelly Yang; and *Drawn Together* by Minh Lê.
Batchelder Award	The Batchelder Award is given to a U.S. publisher for a children's book that originated outside of the United States and was originally written in a language other than English. Winners include *The Fox on the Swing* by Evelina Daciūtė; *The Murderer's Ape*, written and illustrated by Jakob Wegelius; and *Cry, Heart, But Never Break* by Glenn Ringtved.
Coretta Scott King Award	This award is given to authors and illustrators of books that celebrate and show appreciation for African American culture, as well as honor universal human values. Winners include *Piecing Me Together* by Renée Watson and *Out of Wonder: Poems Celebrating Poets*, illustrated by Ekua Holmes and written by Kwame Alexander.
Walter Dean Myers Award for Outstanding Children's Literature	This award is given to books that promote a commitment to showing children of many diverse groups. Winners include *Ghost Boys* by Jewell Parker Rhodes and *Long Way Down* by Jason Reynolds.
Dolly Gray Children's Literature Award	Sponsored by the Council for Exceptional Children, this award is given to books that appropriately portray individuals with developmental disabilities.
Stonewall Book Award	This award is given to books relating to the gay, lesbian, bisexual, and transgender experience.

RANDOLPH CALDECOTT MEDAL

The Caldecott Medal was named in honor of 19th-century English illustrator Randolph Caldecott. It is awarded annually by the Association for Library Service to Children, a division of the American Library Association, to the artist of the most distinguished American picture book for children. Caldecott-awarded books receive this distinct honor. Honor books that are part of the final runner-up list are also designated in this award. Past winners include:

Caldecott-Awarded Books

Hello Lighthouse by Sophie Blackall
Wolf in the Snow by Matthew Cordell
Radiant Child: The Story of Young Artist Jean-Michel Basquiat by Javaka Steptoe
Finding Winnie: The True Story of the World's Most Famous Bear by Lindsay Mattick
The Adventures of Beekle: The Unimaginary Friend by Dan Santat

JOHN NEWBERY AWARD

The Newbery Award is the oldest children's book award in the world. Its criteria, as well as its long history, continue to make it the best known and most discussed children's book award in this country. Books receiving the Newbery Award are honored for their interpretation of the theme or concept; presentation of information, including accuracy, clarity, and organization; development of plot; delineation of characters; delineation of setting; appropriateness of style for literary quality; and the quality of presentation for children. Past winners include:

Newbery-Awarded Books

Merci Suárez Changes Gears by Meg Medina
Hello Universe by Erin Entrada Kelly
The Girl Who Drank the Moon by Kelly Barnhill
Last Stop on Market Street by Matt de la Peña
The Crossover by Kwame Alexander

ORBIS PICTUS AWARD

This annual award promotes and recognizes excellence in nonfiction writing for children. The award commemorates the work of Johannes Amos Comenius, whose book, *Orbis Pictus—The World in Pictures* (1657), is considered to be the first illustrated book created for children. Past winners include:

Between the Lines: How Ernie Barnes Went from Football Field to the Art Gallery by Sandra Neil Wallace
Grand Canyon by Jason Chin
Some Writer!: The Story of E. B. White by Melissa Sweet
Drowned City: Hurricane Katrina & New Orleans by Don Brown
The Family Romanov: Murder, Rebellion & the Fall of Imperial Russia by Candace Fleming

Popular Series Books

Series	Author	Interest level
Pete the Cat	James Dean and Eric Litwin	Ages 3+
Clifford	Norman Bridwell	Ages 5+
Don't Let the Pigeon	Mo Willems	Ages 5+
Elephant and Piggy	Mo Willems	Ages 5+
Who Was/Where Was series	Various authors	Ages 5+
Lola Levine	Monica Brown	Ages 6+
Captain Underpants	Dav Pilkey	Ages 8+
Lunch Lady	Jarret J. Krosoczka	Ages 8+
Lotus Lane	Kyla May	Ages 8+
Amulet	Kazu Kibuishi	Ages 8+
Stink	Megan McDonald	Ages 8+
Big Nate	Lincoln Peirce	Ages 8+
Hamster Princess	Ursula Vernon	Ages 8+
Diary of a Wimpy Kid	Jeff Kinney	Ages 8+
39 Clues	Rick Riordan	Ages 8+
Harry Potter	J. K. Rowling	Ages 10+
The Treehouse books	Andy Griffiths and Terry Denton	Ages 10+
I Survived	Lauren Tarshis	Ages 10+
Hunger Games	Suzanne Collins	Ages 10+
The Maze Runner	James Dashner	Ages 10+
Arc of a Scythe	Neal Shusterman	Ages 10+
Percy Jackson and the Olympians	Rick Riordian	Ages 10+

APPENDIX F

Book Club Choices

Elementary School Choices

The One and Only Ivan by Katherine Applegate
El Deafo by CeCe Bell
The War That Saved My Life by Kimberly Bradley
New Kid by Jerry Craft
Refugee by Alan Gratz
The Apothecary by Maile Malloy

Young Adult Choices

The Crossover by Kwame Alexander
A Good Girl's Guide to Murder by Holly Jackson
Reverie by Ryan La Sala
White Bird by R. J. Palacio
They Called Us Enemy by George Takei
The Book Thief by Markus Zusak

Children's and Teen Choice Book Awards

The Children's and Teen Choice Book Awards are the only national book awards program in which kids select the winners.

Title and author	Interest level
I Say Ooh You Say Aah by John Kane	K–2
Poor Louie by Tony Lucile	K–2
Back to the Future by Robert Zemeckis and Bob Gale	3–4
Fifty Wacky Things Animals Do by Tricia Martineau Wagner	3–4
Ghost Boys by Jewell Parker Rhodes	5–6
The Losers Club by Andrew Clements	5–6
The Hate U Give by Angie Thomas	YA
The Prince and the Dressmaker by Jen Wang	YA

Visit the Children's Book Council website (*www.cbcbooks.org*) for more winners and honor books.

References

Afflerbach, P., & Cho, B. Y. (2009). Identifying and describing constructively responsive comprehension strategies in new and traditional forms of reading. In S. E. Israel & G. G. Duffy (Eds.), *Handbook of research on reading comprehension*, 69–90. New York: Guilford Press.

Afflerbach, P., & Meuwissen, K. (2005). Middle school self-assessment. In S. Israel, C. C. Block, K. Bauserman, & K. Kinnucan-Welsch (Eds.), *Metacognition in literacy learning* (pp. 141–164). Mahwah, NJ: Erlbaum.

Allen, J. (2006). Too little or too much? What do we know about making vocabulary instruction meaningful. *Voices from the Middle, 13*(4), 16–19.

Allen, J. (2007). *Inside words: Tools for teaching academic vocabulary grades 4–12.* Portland, ME: Stenhouse.

Allington, R. (2012). *What really matters for struggling readers* (3rd ed.). Boston: Pearson.

Allington, R. L., & Cunningham, P. (2015). *Schools that work: Where all children read and write* (3rd ed.). Boston: Pearson.

Allington, R. L., & Johnston, P. H. (2002). *Reading to learn: Lessons from exemplary fourth-grade classrooms.* New York: Guilford Press.

Allington, R. L., & McGill-Franzen, A. (2018). *Summer reading: Closing the rich/poor reading achievement gap.* New York: Teachers College Press.

Allington, R. L., McGill-Franzen, A., Camilli, G., Williams, L., Graff, J., Zeig, J., . . . Nowak, R. (2010). Addressing summer reading setback among economically disadvantaged elementary students. *Reading Psychology, 31*(5), 411–427.

Alvermann, D. E. (2001). Reading adolescents' reading identities: Looking back to see ahead. *Journal of Adolescent and Adult Literacy, 44*(8), 676–690.

Alvermann, D. E. (2012). Is there a place for popular culture in curriculum and classroom instruction? *Curriculum and Instruction, 2,* 211–228.

American Indian Literature Association. (n.d.). *American Indian Youth Literature Award.* Retrieved from *https://ailanet.org/activities/american-indian-youth-literature-award.*

Anti-Defamation League. (n.d.). *Assessing children's literature.* Retrieved from *www.adl.org/education/resources/tools-and-strategies/assessing-childrens-literature.*

Applebee, A. N. (1994). Toward thoughtful curriculum: Fostering discipline-based conversation. *The English Journal, 83*(3), 45–52.

Au, K. H. (1993). *Literacy instruction in multicultural settings*. Belmont, CA: Wadsworth.

Au, K. H. (2015). Isn't culturally responsive instruction just good teaching? In W. C. Parker (Ed.), *Social studies today* (2nd ed., pp. 95–104). New York: Routledge.

Au, K. H., & Mason, J. M. (1983). Cultural congruence in classroom participation structures: Achieving a balance of rights. *Discourse Processes, 6*(2), 145–167.

Aukerman, M. (2008). In praise of wiggle room: Locating comprehension in unlikely places. *Language Arts, 86*(1), 52–60.

Aukerman, M. (2013). Rereading comprehension pedagogies: Toward a dialogic teaching ethic that honors student sense making. *Dialogic Pedagogy, 1*, A1–A31.

Bandura, A. (1977). Self-efficacy: Toward a unifying theory of behavioral change. *Psychological Review, 84*(2), 191–215.

Banks, J., Cochran-Smith, M., Moll, L., Richert, A., Zeichner, K., LePage, P., . . . McDonald, M. (2005). Teaching diverse learners. In L. Darling-Hammand & J. Bransford (Eds.), *Preparing teachers for a changing world: What teachers should learn and be able to do* (pp. 232–274). San Francisco: Jossey-Bass.

Banks-Wallace, J. (2002). Talk that talk: Storytelling and analysis rooted in African American oral tradition. *Qualitative Health Research, 12*(3), 410–426.

Beck, I., & McKeown, M. (1991). Conditions of vocabulary acquisition. In R. Barr, M. Kamil, P. Mosenthal, & P. D. Pearson (Eds.), *Handbook of reading research* (Vol 2, pp. 789–814). New York: Longman.

Beers, K., & Probst, J. (2017) *Disruptive thinking: Why how we read matters*. New York: Scholastic.

Bersh, L. C. (2013). The curricular value of teaching about immigration through picture book thematic text sets. *The Social Studies, 104*(2), 47–56.

Bishop, R. S. (1990). Mirrors, windows, and sliding glass doors. *Perspectives: Choosing and using books for the classroom, 6*(3), 9–12.

Bishop, R. S. (1992). Multicultural literature for children: Making informed choices. In V. J. Harris (Ed.), *Teaching multicultural literature in grades K–8* (pp. 37–53). Norwood, MA: Christopher-Gordon.

Bishop, R. S. (2009). Surveying the hopescape. In J. Hoffman & Y. Goodman (Eds.), *Changing literacies for changing times* (pp. 71–80). New York: Routledge.

Black, P., & Wiliam, D. (1998). Assessment and classroom learning. *Assessment in Education: Principles, Policy & Practice, 5*(1), 7–74.

Block, C. C., & Pressley, M. (Eds.). (2002). *Comprehension instruction: Research-based best practices*. New York: Guilford Press.

Blumenfeld, P. C., Soloway, E., Marx, R. W., Krajcik, J. S., Guzdial, M., & Palincsar, A. (1991). Motivating project-based learning: Sustaining the doing, supporting the learning. *Educational Psychologist, 26*(3–4), 369–398.

Brenner, D., & Hiebert, E. H. (2010). If I follow the teachers' editions, isn't that enough? Analyzing reading volume in six core reading programs. *The Elementary School Journal, 110*(3), 347–363.

Brenner, D., Hiebert, E. H., & Tompkins, R. (2009). Reading in core programs. In E. H. Hiebert (Ed.), *Reading more, reading better* (pp. 118–140). New York: Guilford Press.

Brophy, J. (1983). Conceptualizing student motivation. *Educational Psychologist, 18*(3), 200–215.

Bullough, R. V., & Hall-Kenyon, K. M. (2011). The call to teach and teacher hopefulness. *Teacher Development: An International Journal of Teachers' Professional Development, 15*, 127–140.

Caldwell, J., & Leslie, L. (2012*). Intervention strategies to follow informal reading inventory assessment: So what do I do now?* Boston: Pearson.

Cazden, C. B. (2001). *Classroom discourse: The language of teaching and learning.* Portsmouth, NH: Heinemann.

Cochran-Smith, M., & Lytle, S. (2009). Teacher research as stance. In S. Noffke & B. Somekh (Eds.), *The Sage handbook of educational action research* (pp. 39–49). Los Angeles: Sage.

Collins, K., & Ferri, B. (2016). Literacy education and disability studies: Reenvisioning struggling students. *Journal of Adolescent and Adult Literacy, 60*(1), 7–12.

Crone, D. A., & Whitehurst, G. J. (1999). Age and schooling effects on emergent literacy and early reading skills. *Journal of Educational Psychology, 91*(4), 604–614.

Cruz, B., & Thornton, S. (2009). Social studies for English language learners: Teaching social studies that matters. *Social Education, 73*(6), 271–274.

Cuban, L. (2013). *Inside the black box of classroom practice: Change without reform in American education.* Cambridge, MA: Harvard Education Press.

Cunningham, P., & Allington, R. (2007). *Classrooms that work: They can all read and write* (6th ed.). Boston: Pearson.

Daniels, H. (2002). *Literature circles: Voice and choice in book clubs and reading groups.* Portland, ME: Stenhouse.

Darling Hammond, L., & Bransford, J. (Eds.). (2005). *What teachers should learn and be able to do.* San Francisco: Jossey-Bass.

DÁvila, D. S., Melilli, A., Canady, F., Dunham, H., Alexander, K., & Li, K. (2019). Picture books and the cycle of grief. *Journal of Children's Literature, 45*(2), 88–96.

Dewey, J. (1933). *How we think: A restatement of the relation of reflective thinking to the educative process.* Boston: DC Heath.

Duffy, G. G. (2002). Visioning and the development of outstanding teachers. *Reading Research and Instruction, 41*(4), 331–344.

Duke, N. K. (2000). 3.6 minutes per day: The scarcity of informational texts in first grade. *Reading Research Quarterly, 35*(2), 202–224.

Duke, N. K. (2016). Project-based instruction: A great match for informational texts. *American Educator,* pp. 4–42. Retrieved from *https://www.lucasedresearch.org/wp-content/uploads/2021/02/Project_Based_Instruction_Info_Text.pdf.*

Duke, N. K., Cervetti, G. N., & Wise, C. N. (2018). Learning from exemplary teachers of literacy. *The Reading Teacher, 71*(4), 395–400.

Duke, N. K., Halvorsen, A. L., & Strachan, S. L. (2016). Project-based learning not just for STEM anymore. *Phi Delta Kappan, 98*(1), 14–19.

Duke, N. K., Pearson, P. D., Strachan, S. L., & Billman, A. K. (2011). Essential elements of fostering and teaching reading comprehension. In S. J. Samuels & A. E. Farstrup (Eds.), *What research has to say about reading instruction* (4th ed., pp. 286–314). Newark, DE: International Reading Association.

Dutro, E. (2008). "That's why I was crying on this book": Trauma as testimony in responses to literature. *Changing English, 15*(4), 423–434.

Dyson, A. H. (2003). "Welcome to the jam": Popular culture, school literacy, and the making of childhoods. *Harvard Educational Review, 73*(3), 328–361.

Dyson, A. H. (2020). "This isn't my real writing": The fate of children's agency in too-tight curricula. *Theory Into Practice, 59*(2), 119–127.

Eccles, J. S., & Wigfield, A. (2002). Motivational beliefs, values, and goals. *Annual Review of Psychology, 53*(1), 109–132.

Epstein, T. (2009). *Interpreting national history.* New York: Routledge.

Ericcson, K. A., Prietula, M. J., & Cokely, E. T. (2007). The making of an expert. *Harvard Business Review, 85*(7/8), 114–121.

Fink, J. (n.d.). Genius hour in the classroom. Retrieved from *www.scholastic.com/teachers/ articles/18-19/genius-hour-in-the-classroom.*

Fisher, D., & Frey, N. (2008). *Word wise and content rich: Five essential steps to teaching academic vocabulary.* Portsmouth, NH: Heinemann.

Folk, W., & Palmer, T. (2016). Light, color, vision, optics! A text set for grades 6–8. *Science Scope, 39*(8), 39–44.

Freire, P. (1970). *Pedagogy of the oppressed* (M. B. Ramos, Trans.). New York: Continuum.

Gallagher, K. (2011) *Write like this.* Portland, ME: Stenhouse.

Gallagher, K., & Kittle, P. (2018). *180 days: Two teachers and the quest to engage and empower adolescents.* Portsmouth, NH: Heinemann.

Gambrell, L. B. (2011). Seven rules of engagement: What's most important to know about motivation to read. *The Reading Teacher, 65*(3), 172–178.

Gambrell, L. B. (2015). Getting students hooked on the reading habit. *The Reading Teacher, 69*(3), 259–263.

Gambrell, L. B., Malloy, J. A., & Mazzoni, S. A. (2011). Evidence-based best practices for comprehensive literacy instruction. In L. B. Gambrell & L. M. Morrow (Eds.), *Best practices in literacy instruction* (4th ed., pp. 11–36). New York: Guilford Press.

Garcia, A., & O'Donnell-Allen, C. (2015). *Pose, wobble, flow: A culturally proactive approach to literacy instruction.* New York: Teachers College Press.

García, O., & Wei, L. (2014). Translanguaging and education. In *Translanguaging: Language, bilingualism and education* (pp. 63–77). London: Macmillan.

Gay, G. (2000). *Culturally responsive teaching: Theory, practice, and research.* New York: Teachers College Press.

Gay, G. (2010). Acting on beliefs in teacher education for cultural diversity. *Journal of Teacher Education, 61*(1–2), 143–152.

Gee, J. P. (2012). *Situated language and learning: A critique of traditional schooling.* New York: Routledge.

Goodley, D. (2007). Towards socially just pedagogies: Deleuzoguattarian critical disability studies. *International Journal of Inclusive Education, 11*(3), 317–334.

Goodwin, A. P., & Jiménez, R. (2016). TRANSLATE: New strategic approaches for English learners. *The Reading Teacher, 69*(6), 621–625.

Grant, T. (2011). Brian Selznick's "Wonderstruck" is a worthy family tradition. Retrieved from *www.washingtonpost.com/lifestyle/advice/brian-selznicks-wonderstruck-is-a-worthy-family-tradition/2011/11/20/gIQAOOgPCO_story.html.*

Guthrie, J. T. (2008). *Engaging adolescents in reading.* New York: Corwin Press.

Guthrie, J. T., Schafer, W. D., & Huang, C. W. (2001). Benefits of opportunity to read and balanced instruction on the NAEP. *Journal of Educational Research, 94*(3), 145–162.

Guthrie, J. T., & Wigfield, A. (2000). Engagement and motivation in reading. In M. L. Kamil, P. B. Mosenthal, P. D. Pearson, & R. Barr (Eds.), *Handbook of reading research* (Vol. 3, pp. 403–422). New York: Erlbaum.

Guthrie, J. T., Wigfield, A., & You, W. (2012). Instructional contexts for engagement and achievement in reading. In S. Christenson, A. Reschly, & C. Wylie (Eds.), *Handbook of research on student engagement* (pp. 601–634). Boston: Springer.

Hartman, D. K., Morsink, P. M., & Zheng, J. (2010). From print to pixels: The evolution of cognitive conceptions of reading comprehension. In E. A. Baker (Ed.), *The new literacies: Multiple perspectives on research and practice* (pp. 131–164). New York: Guilford Press.

Heafner, T. L., & Massey, D. D. (2012). *Targeted vocabulary instruction in social studies: Tools for academic achievement.* Culver City, CA: Social Studies School Service.

Hebert, M., Bohaty, J. J., Nelson, J. R., & Brown, J. (2016). The effects of text structure instruction on expository reading comprehension: A meta-analysis. *Journal of Educational Psychology, 108*(5), 609–629.

Herman, P. A., Anderson, R. C., Pearson, P. D., & Nagy, W. E. (1987). Incidental acquisition of word meaning from expositions with varied text features. *Reading Research Quarterly, 22*(3), 263–284.

Hiebert, E. H. (2014). *The forgotten reading proficiency: Stamina in silent reading.* Retrieved from *http://sites.bu.edu/summerliteracyinstitute/files/2015/04/HiebertE-The-forgotten-reading-proficiency.pdf* .

Hiebert, E. H., & Martin, L. (2009). Opportunity to read: A critical but neglected construct in reading instruction. In E. H. Hiebert (Ed.), *Reading more, reading better* (pp. 3–29). New York: Guilford Press.

Hinchman, K. A., & Moore, D. W. (2013). Close reading: A cautionary interpretation. *Journal of Adolescent & Adult Literacy, 56*(6), 441–450.

Holland, D., Lachicotte, W., Skinner, D., & Cain, C. (1998). *Identity and agency in cultural worlds.* Cambridge, MA: Harvard University Press.

Huck, C. (1997). *Children's literature in the elementary school.* New York: Brown & Benchmark.

International Literacy Association. (2017). *Standards for the preparation of literacy professionals.* Retrieved from *https://literacyworldwide.org/get-resources/standards/standards-2017.*

Ivey, G. (2014). The social side of engaged reading for young adolescents. *The Reading Teacher, 68*(3), 165–171.

Ivey, G., & Fisher, D. (2006). When thinking skills trump reading skills. *Educational Leadership, 64*(2), 16–21.

Ivey, G., & Johnston, P. H. (2013). Engagement with young adult literature: Outcomes and processes. *Reading Research Quarterly, 48*(3), 255–275.

Ivey, G., & Johnston, P. (2015). Engaged reading as collaborative transformative practice. *Journal of Literacy Research, 47*(3) 297–327.

Jang, B. G., Conradi, K., McKenna, M. C., & Jones, J. S. (2015). Motivation. *The Reading Teacher, 69*(2), 239–247.

Javorsky, K., & Trainin, G. (2014). Teaching young readers to navigate a digital story when rules keep changing. *The Reading Teacher, 67*(8), 606–618.

Johnson, N. J., Koss, M. D., & Martinez, M. (2018). Through the sliding glass door: #EmpowerTheReader. *The Reading Teacher, 71*(5), 569–577.

Johnston, P. H. (2004). *Choice words: How our language affects children's learning.* Portland, ME: Stenhouse.

Johnston, P. H., Champeau, K., Hartwig, A., Helmer, S., Komar, M., Krueger, T., & McCarthy, L. (2020). *Engaging literate minds: Developing children's social, emotional, and intellectual lives, K–3.* Portland, ME: Stenhouse.

Johnston, P., & Costello, P. (2005). Principles for literacy assessment. *Reading Research Quarterly, 40*(2), 256–267.

Jones, B. F., Rasmussen, C. M., & Moffitt, M. C. (1997). *Real-life problem solving: A collaborative approach to interdisciplinary learning.* Washington, DC: American Psychological Association.

Kamil, M. L. (2016). Common Core State Standards and adaptive teaching. *Theory Into Practice, 55*(3), 234–241.

Kelley, J. E., Stair, M., & Price, P. G. (2013). Anthropomorphic veneers in Voices in the Park: Questioning the master narratives through a socio-historical analysis of images and text. *The Dragon Lode, 31*(2), 44–53.

Kena, G., Musu-Gillette, L., Robinson, J., Wang, X., Rathbun, A., Zhang, J., . . . Dunlop Velez, E. (2015). *The condition of education 2015* (NCES 2015-144). Washington, DC: U.S. Department of Education, National Center for Education Statistics.

Klarer, M. (2004). *An introduction to English and American literary studies* (2nd ed.). New York: Routledge.

Koltz, J., & Kersten-Parrish, S. (2020). Using children's picturebooks to facilitate restorative justice discussion. *The Reading Teacher, 73*(5), 637–645.

Kondo, M. (2014). *The life-changing magic of tidying up.* New York: Ten Speed Press.

Kovach, M. (2010). Conversational method in Indigenous research. *First Peoples Child and Family Review, 14*(1), 123–136.

Ladson-Billings, G. (2005). *Beyond the big house: African American educators on teacher education.* New York: Teacher College Press.

Ladson-Billings, G., & Tate, W. F. (Eds.). (2006). *Education research in the public interest: Social justice, action, and policy.* New York: Teachers College Press.

Lahey, J. (2015). The role of adult mentorship in helping children deal with trauma. Retrieved from *www.theatlantic.com/education/archive/2015/06/cultivating-hope-in-kids-whove-grown-up-without-it/395438.*

Layne, S. L. (2009). *Igniting a passion for reading: Successful strategies for building lifetime readers.* Portland, ME: Stenhouse.

Lazarus, R. S. (1999). Hope: An emotion and a vital coping resource against despair. *Social Research,* 653–678.

Learned, J. E. (2016). "Feeling like I'm slow because I'm in this class": Secondary school contexts and the identification and construction of struggling readers. *Reading Research Quarterly, 51*(4), 367–371.

Lin, G. (2016). *The windows and mirrors of your child's bookshelf* [TEDtalk]. Retrieved from *www.youtube.com/watch?v=_wQ8wiV3FVo.*

Lucas, C. V., Teixeira, D., Soares, L., & Oliveira, F. (2019). Bibliotherapy as a hope-building tool in educational settings. *Journal of Poetry Therapy, 32*(4), 199–213.

Lupo, S. M., Berry, A., Thacker, E., Sawyer, A., & Merritt, J. (2019). Rethinking text sets to support knowledge building and interdisciplinary learning. *The Reading Teacher, 73*(4), 513–524.

Lupo, S., Mitnick-Wilson, A., & Massey, D. D. (2016, December). *Painting a picture of adolescent readers: Implications and challenges of assessment.* Symposium conducted at the meeting of the Literacy Research Association, Nashville, TN.

Lysaker, J. T., Tonge, C., Gauson, D., & Miller, A. (2011). Reading and social imagination: What relationally oriented reading instruction can do for children. *Reading Psychology, 32*(6), 520–566.

Madda, C. L., Griffo, V. B., Pearson, P. D., & Raphael, T. E. (2011). Balance in comprehensive literacy instruction: Evolving conceptions. In L. M. Morrow & L. B. Gambrell (Eds.), *Best practices in literacy instruction* (4th ed., pp. 37–63). New York: Guilford Press.

Maholmes, V. (2014). *Fostering resilience and well-being in children and families in poverty: Why hope still matters.* Oxford, UK: Oxford University Press.

Malloy, J. A., Parsons, A. W., Marinak, B. A., Applegate, A. J., Applegate, M. D., Reutzel, D. R., . . . Gambrell, L. B. (2017). Assessing (and addressing!) motivation to read fiction and nonfiction. *The Reading Teacher, 71*(3), 309–325.

Marinak, B. A., & Gambrell, L. B. (2016). *No more reading for junk: Best practices for motivating readers.* Portsmouth, NH: Heinemann.

Marzano, R. (2004). *Building background knowledge for academic achievement: Research on what works in schools.* Alexandrea, VA: Association for Supervision and Curriculum Development.

Massey, D. D. (2007). "The Discovery Channel said so!" and other barriers to comprehension. *The Reading Teacher, 60,* 656–666.

Massey, D. D. (2015, December). *Tutoring to support understanding and achievement: What tutors and tutees learn.* Symposium conducted at the meeting of the Literacy Research Association, Carlsbad, CA.

Massey, D. D., Miller, S. D., & Metzger, S. (2017, December). *Reading is something I teach, not something they do.* Paper presented at the meeting of the Literacy Research Association, Tampa, FL.

McNamara, D. S., Floyd, R. G., Best, R., & Louwerse, M. (2004). World knowledge driving young readers' comprehension difficulties. In Y. B. Yasmin, W. A. Sandoval, N. Edyedy, A. S. Nixon, & F. Herrera (Eds.), *Proceedings of the 6th International Conference on the Learning Sciences* (pp. 326–333). Mahwah, NJ: Erlbaum.

Mendoza, E., Kirshner, B., & Gutiérrez, K. D. (Eds.). (2018). *Power, equity and (re) design: Bridging learning and critical theories in learning ecologies for youth.* Charlotte, NC: Information Age.

Meyer, B. J., Brandt, D. M., & Bluth, G. J. (1980). Use of top-level structure in text: Key for reading comprehension of ninth-grade students. *Reading Research Quarterly, 16,* 72–103.

Miller, D. (2013). *Reading with meaning* (2nd ed.). Portland, ME: Stenhouse.

Moje, E. B., Ciechanowski, K. M., Kramer, K., Ellis, L., Carrillo, R., & Collazo, T. (2004). Working toward third space in content area literacy: An examination of everyday funds of knowledge and discourse. *Reading Research Quarterly, 39*(1), 38–70.

Moll, L. C., Amanti, C., Neff, D., & Gonzalez, N. (1992). Funds of knowledge for teaching: Using a qualitative approach to connect homes and classrooms. *Theory Into Practice, 31*(2), 132–141.

Moodley, T., & Aronstam, S. (2016). *Authentic learning for teaching reading: Foundation phase pre-service student teachers' learning experiences of creating and using digital stories in real classrooms.* Retrieved from *https://files.eric.ed.gov/fulltext/EJ1186977.pdf.*

Morrow, L. M., & Tracey, D. H. (2012). *Lenses on reading: An introduction to theories and models* (2nd ed.). New York: Guilford Press.

Nasir, N. S. (2002). Identity, goals, and learning: Mathematics in cultural practice. *Mathematical Thinking and Learning, 4,* 213–247.

Nasir, N. S., & Cooks, J. (2009). Becoming a hurdler: How learning settings afford identities. *Anthropology and Education Quarterly, 40*(1), 41–61.

National Academies of Sciences, Engineering, and Medicine. (2018). *How people learn II: Learners, contexts, and cultures.* Washington, DC: National Academies Press.

National Governors Association Center for Best Practices & Council of Chief State School Officers. (2010). *Common Core State Standards.* Washington, DC: Authors.

National Governors Association Center for Best Practices & Council of Chief State School

Officers. (2012). *Revised publishers' criteria for the Common Core State Standards in English Language Arts and Literacy, grades 3–12.* Washington, DC: Authors. Retrieved from *www.corestandards.org/assets/Publishers_Criteria_ for_3-12.pdf.*

New York State Education Department. (n.d.). *EngageNY grade 4 English language arts.* Retrieved from *www.engageny.org/resource/grade-4-english-language-arts.*

Nieto, S. (2000). Placing equity front and center: Some thoughts on transforming teacher education for a new century. *Journal of Teacher Education, 51*(3), 180–187.

No Child Left Behind Act of 2001, Public Law No.107-110, 20 U.S.C. § 6319 (2002).

Ogle, D., Klemp, R. M., & McBride, B. (2007). *Building literacy in social studies: Strategies for improving comprehension and critical thinking.* Alexandra, VA: ASCD.

Pahl, K., & Roswell, J. (2013). Artifactual literacies. In J. Larson & J. Marsh (Eds.), *The Sage handbook of early childhood literacy* (2nd ed., pp. 263–278). Los Angeles: Sage.

Paquette, K. R. (2007). Encouraging primary students' writing through children's literature. *Early Childhood Education Journal, 35*(2), 155–165.

Paris, D., & Alim, H. S. (Eds.). (2017). *Culturally sustaining pedagogies: Teaching and learning for justice in a changing world.* New York: Teachers College Press.

Paul, P. (2017). *My life with Bob.* New York: Holt.

Pearson, P. D., & Cervetti, G. N. (2017). The roots of reading comprehension instruction. In S. E. Israel (Ed.), *Handbook of research on reading comprehension* (2nd ed., pp. 12–56). New York: Guilford Press.

Phillips, E. C., & Sturm, B. W. (2013) Do picture books about starting kindergarten portray the kindergarten experience in developmentally appropriate ways? *Early Childhood Education Journal 41*(6), 465–475.

Pressley, M., & Afflerbach, P. (1995). *Verbal protocols of reading.* Hillsdale, NJ: Erlbaum.

Pressley, M., Allington, R. L., Wharton-McDonald, R., Block, C. C., & Morrow, L. M. (2001). *Learning to read: Lessons from exemplary first-grade classrooms.* New York: Guilford Press.

Pyle, N., Vasquez, A. C., Lignugaris/Kraft, B., Gillam, S. L., Reutzel, D. R., Olszewski, A., . . . Pyle, D. (2017). Effects of expository text structure interventions on comprehension: A meta-analysis. *Reading Research Quarterly, 52*(4), 469–501.

Ray, K. W. (1999). *Wondrous words: Writers and writing in the elementary classroom.* Urbana, IL: National Council of Teachers of English.

Reading Excellence Act of 1998, Public Law 105-277, Div. A, Sec. 101(f) (title VIII), 112 Stat. 2681-337, 2681-391 *et. seq.* United States Department of Education, 2002. *Reading Excellence Program: Legislation.* Retrieved February 26, 2020, from *www2.ed.gov/pubs/ promisinginitiatives/rea.html.*

Reutzel, D. R., Fawson, P. C., & Smith, J. A. (2008). Reconsidering silent sustained reading: An exploratory study of scaffolded silent reading. *Journal of Educational Research, 102*(1), 37–50.

Robinson, H., Monroe, M., Artley, A. S., Huck, C. S., Aaron, I., & Weintraub, S. (Eds.). (1965). *Ventures: Teachers edition book 4.* Chicago: Scott Foresman.

Rodriguez, N. N., & Kim, E. J. (2018). In search of mirrors: An Asian critical race theory content analysis of Asian American picturebooks from 2007 to 2017. *Journal of Children's Literature, 44*(2), 17–30.

Rosenblatt, L. M. (1978). *The reader, the text, the poem.* Carbondale, IL: Southern Illinois University Press.

Rosenblatt, L. M. (1988). *Writing and reading: The transactional theory* (Center for the Study of Reading Technical Report No. 416). Champaign, IL: University of Illinois at Urbana–Champaign.

Rosenblatt, L. (1994). The transactional theory of reading and writing. In R. B. Ruddell, M. R. Ruddell, & H. Singer (Eds.), *Theoretical models and processes of reading* (4th ed., pp. 1057–1092). Newark, DE: International Reading Association.

Santori, D. M. (2008). *"Sense-making—The heart of the matter": Exploring reading comprehension in various participation structures.* Doctoral dissertation, University of Pennsylvania. Available from *ProQuest AAI3322286. https://repository.upenn.edu/dissertations/AAI3322286*

Schunk, D. (1984). The self-efficacy perspective on achievement behavior. *Educational Psychologist, 19,* 199–218.

Schunk, D. (1989). Social cognitive theory and self-regulated learning. In B. J. Zimmerman & D. H. Schunk (Eds.), *Self-regulated learning and academic achievement: Theory, research, and practice* (pp. 83–110). New York: Springer-Verlag.

Selin, E., & Graube, K. (2017, June). *Reading aloud to children in hospital: Bibliotherapy as a community builder.* Paper presented at the European Association for Health Information and Libraries Conference. Retrieved from *http://library.ifla.org/1784/1/138-selin-en.pdf.*

Serafini, F. (1993). Informing our practice: Modernist, transactional, and critical perspectives on children's literature and reading instruction. *Reading Online, 6*(6). Retrieved from *http://frankserafini.com/publications/serafini—informing-practi.pdf.*

Serafini, F. (2009). Understanding visual images in picturebooks. In J. Evans (Ed.), *Talking beyond the page: Reading and responding to picturebooks* (pp. 10–25). New York: Routledge.

Shanahan, T. (2017). What is close reading? Retrieved from *https://shanahanonliteracy.com/blog/what-is-close-reading.*

Short, K., Harste, J., & Burke, C. (1996). *Creating classrooms for authors and inquirers.* Portsmouth, NH: Heinemann.

Sipe, L. R. (2000). The construction of literary understanding by first and second graders in oral response to picture storybook read-alouds. *Reading Research Quarterly, 35*(2), 252–275.

Smith, F. (2006). *Reading without nonsense* (4th ed.). Cambridge, MA: Harvard University Press.

Smith, M. (2017). Genius hour in elementary school. Retrieved from *www.edutopia.org/article/genius-hour-elementary-school.*

Snow, C. (2002). *Reading for understanding: Toward an R&D program in reading comprehension.* Santa Monica, CA: Rand Corporation.

Spandel, V. (2005). *Creating writers: Through 6-trait writing assessment and instruction.* Boston: Allyn & Bacon.

Spencer, J. (2017). The genius of design. *Educational Leadership, 74*(6), 16–21.

Spencer, L. M., Jr., & Spencer, S. M. (1993). *Competence at work: Models for superior performance.* New York: Wiley.

Stahl, S. A., Hare, V. C., Sinatra, R., & Gregory, J. F. (1991). Defining the role of prior knowledge and vocabulary in reading comprehension: The retiring of number 41. *Journal of Reading Behavior, 23*(4), 487–508.

Stahl, S. A., & Nagy, W. E. (2006). *The literacy teaching series. Teaching word meanings.* Mahwah, NJ: Erlbaum.

Tan, E., Barton, A., Kang, H., & O'Neill, T. (2013). Desiring a career in STEM-related fields: How middle school girls articulate and negotiate identities-in-practice in science. *Journal of Research in Science Teaching, 50,* 1143–1179.

Thompson, G., Madhuri, M., & Taylor, D. (2008). How the Accelerated Reader program can become counterproductive for high school students. *Journal of Adolescent and Adult Literacy, 51*(7), 550–560.

U.S. Department of Education. (2009, November). *Race to the Top program executive summary.* Retrieved from *www.ed.gov/programs/racetothetop/executive-summary.pdf.*

Vadeboncoeur, J. A., Vellos, R. E., & Goessling, K. P. (2011). Learning as (one part) identity construction: Educational implications of a sociocultural perspective. In D. McInerney, R. A. Walter, & G. A. D. Liem (Eds.), *Sociocultural theories of learning and motivation: Looking back, looking forward* (Vol.10, pp. 223–251). Greenwich, CT: Information Age.

van der Veen, C., van Kruistum, C., & Michaels, S. (2015). Productive classroom dialogue as an activity of shared thinking and communicating: A commentary on Marsal. *Mind, Culture, and Activity, 22*(4), 320–325.

Vasquez, V. M. (2014). *Negotiating critical literacies with young children.* New York: Routledge.

Vaughn, M. (2014). The role of student agency: Exploring openings during literacy instruction. *Teaching and Learning, 28*(1), 4–16.

Vaughn, M. (2016). Re-envisioning literacy in a teacher inquiry group in a Native American context. *Literacy Research and Instruction, 55*(1), 24–47.

Vaughn, M. (2018). Making sense of student agency in the early grades. *Phi Delta Kappan, 99*(7), 62–66.

Vaughn, M., & Massey, D. (2017). This is the first book I ever read that I couldn't put down: Structuring authentic opportunities in literacy methods for preservice teachers. *Journal of Literacy Practice and Research, 43*(1), 34–40.

Vaughn, M., & Massey, D. D. (2019). Tackle reading: Putting purposeful reading back into literacy instruction. *Literacy Today, 37*(3), 10–11.

Vaughn, M., Parsons, S., Gallagher, M., & Branen, J. (2016). Teachers' adaptive instruction supporting students' literacy learning. *The Reading Teacher, 69,* 539–547.

Vaughn, M., Parsons, S. A., & Massey, D. (2020). Aligning the science of reading with adaptive teaching. *Reading Research Quarterly, 55*(1), 299–306.

Vaughn, M., Premo, J., Sotirovska, V. V., & Erickson, D. (2020). Evaluating agency in literacy using the student agency profile. *The Reading Teacher, 73*(4), 427–441.

Vygotsky, L. S. (1978). *Mind in society.* Cambridge, MA: Harvard University Press.

Wall, A., Massey, D., & Vaughn, M. (2018). Research summary: Student agency. Retrieved from *www.amle.org/BrowsebyTopic/WhatsNew/WNDet/TabId/270/ArtMID/888/ArticleID/995/Student-Agency.aspx.*

Wee, S. J., Park, S., & Choi, J. S. (2015). Korean culture as portrayed in young children's picture books: The pursuit of cultural authenticity. *Children's Literature in Education 46*(1), 70–87.

West, J. M., & Roberts, K. L. (2016). Caught up in curiosity: Genius hour in the kindergarten classroom. *The Reading Teacher, 70*(2), 227–232.

Wharton-McDonald, R., Pressley, M., & Hampston, J. M. (1998). Literacy instruction in nine first-grade classrooms: Teacher characteristics and student achievement. *The Elementary School Journal, 99*(2), 101–128.

Whitin, P. E. (2009). "Tech-to-stretch": Expanding possibilities for literature response. *The Reading Teacher, 62*(5), 408–418.

Wijekumarn, K., & Beerwinkle, A. (2018). Implementing the text structure strategy in your classroom. Retrieved from *www.readingrockets.org/article/implementing-text-structure-strategy-your-classroom*.

Wilhelm, J. D., & Smith, M. W. (2014). Reading don't fix no Chevys (yet!): Motivating boys in the age of the Common Core. *Journal of Adolescent and Adult Literacy, 58*(4), 273–276.

Williams, J. P. (2018). Text structure instruction: The research is moving forward. *Reading and Writing, 31*(9), 1923–1935.

Wiseman, A. M. (2013). Summer's end and sad goodbyes: Children's picturebooks about death and dying. *Children's Literature in Education, 44*(1), 1–14.

Wolf, M. (2018). *Reader, come home: The reading brain in a digital world.* New York: Harper.

Woodson, J. (n.d.). Frequently asked questions. Retrieved from *www.jacquelinewoodson.com/frequently-asked-questions*.

Zimmerman, B. J. (1989). Models of self-regulated learning and academic achievement. In B. J. Zimmerman & D. H. Schunk (Eds.), *Self-regulated learning and academic achievement: Theory, research, and practice* (pp. 1–25). New York: Springer-Verlag.

Zumbrunn, S., Marrs, S., Broda, M., Ekholm, E., DeBusk-Lane, M., & Jackson, L. (2019). Toward a more complete understanding of writing enjoyment: A mixed methods study of elementary students. *AERA Open, 5*(2), 1–16.

Zwiers, J., & Crawford, M. (2011). *Academic conversations: Classroom talk that fosters critical thinking and content understandings.* Portland, ME: Stenhouse.

Children's Literature

Alexander, K. (2014). *The crossover*. Boston: Houghton Mifflin Harcourt.

Alexander, K. (2018). *Rebound*. Boston: Houghton Mifflin Harcourt.

Applegate, K. (2012). *The one and only Ivan*. New York: HarperCollins.

Applegate, K. (2017). *Wishtree*. New York: Feiwel and Friends.

Barnes, D. (2017). *Crown: Ode to a fresh cut*. Chicago: Bolden Books.

Barnett, M., & Klassen, J. (2012). *Extra yarn*. New York: Balzer + Bray.

Barrett, J., & Barrett, R. (1982). *Cloudy with a chance of meatballs*. New York: Atheneum Books for Young Children.

Basher, S. (2007). *The periodic table: Elements with style*. New York: Kingfisher Books.

Basher, S. (2009). *Rocks and minerals: A gem of a book!* New York: Kingfisher Books.

Becker, A. (2013, 2014, 2015). *Journey, quest, and return: A trilogy*. Somerville, MA: Candlewick Press.

Bell, C. (2014). *El Deafo*. New York: Abrams.

Boothroyd, J. (2010). *Give it a push or pull*. Minneapolis: Lerner.

Bradley, K. (2009). *Forces that make things move*. New York: Paw Prints.

Bradley, K. (2016). *The war that saved my life*. New York: Puffin Books.

Branley, F. (2015). *The moon seems to change*. New York: HarperCollins.

Brown, D. (2015). *Drowned city: Hurricane Katrina and New Orleans*. New York: Houghton Mifflin Harcourt.

Brown, M. W. (1949). *The important book*. New York: Harper & Row.

Brown, M. (2005). *My name is Gabriela*. New York: Scholastic.

Bruchac, J., & London, J. (1992). *Thirteen moons on turtle's back: A Native American year of moons*. New York: PaperStar.

Bunting, E. (2005). *Gleam and glow*. New York: Harcourt Children's Books.

Burns, K. (1999). *Not for ourselves alone: The story of Elizabeth Cady Stanton and Susan B. Anthony*. Excerpts retrieved from *www.pbs.org/kenburns/not-for-ourselves-alone/womens-suffrage*.

Coan, S. (2015). *Pushes and pulls*. Huntington Beach, CA: Teacher Created Materials.

Cowley, J. (1993). *Mrs. Wishy Washy*. New York: Philomel Books.

Craft, J. (2019). *New kid*. New York: Quill Tree Books.

Creech, S. (2001). *Love that dog*. New York: HarperCollins.

Dahl, R. (2009). *The magic finger*. New York: Puffin Books.

Dembicki, M. (2010). *Trickster: Native American tales, a graphic collection*. Golden, CO: Fulcrum Books.

DiCamillo, K. (2016). *Flora & Ulysses*. Somerville, MA: Candlewick Press.

DK. (2015). *When on earth*. New York: DK Children.

DK. (2018). *Timelines of everything*. New York: DK Children.

Ehlert, L. (1989). *Eating the alphabet: Fruits and vegetables from A to Z*. New York: Harcourt Brace.

Ellis, D. (2015). *Parvana's journey*. Toronto: Groundwood Books.

Eulate, A. (2012). *The sky of Afghanistan*. Madrid: Shanghai Chenxi.

Falconer, I. (2010). *Olivia goes to Venice*. New York: Atheneum Books for Young Readers.

Gibbons, G. (2019). *The moon book* (4th ed.). New York: Holiday House.

Guojing. (2015). *The only child*. New York: Schwartz & Wade.

Horton, J. (1999). *Halloween hoots and howls*. New York: Holt.

Hosseini, K. (2011). *The kite runner: Graphic novel*. London: Bloomsbury.

Hunter, E. (2021). *Warriors: The broken code #5: The place of stars*. New York: HarperCollins.

Jenkins, S. (2004). *Hottest, coldest, highest, deepest*. New York: Houghton Mifflin.

Jenkins, S. (2011). *Actual size*. New York: Houghton Mifflin.

Katz, J. (2001). *Take me out of the bathtub*. New York: Margaret McElderry Books.

Kenney, K. (2014a). *U.S. history through infographics*. New York: Lerner Classroom.

Kenney, K. (2014b). *Economics through infographics*. New York: Lerner Classroom.

Kinney, J. (2007). *Diary of a wimpy kid*. New York: Amulet.

Kuntz, D., & Shrodes, A. (2017). *Lost and found cat: The true story of Kunkush's incredible journey*. New York: Random House Children's Books.

Lee, S. (2008). *Wave*. San Francisco: Chronicle Books.

Levinson, C., (2017). *The youngest marcher: The story of Audrey Faye Hendricks, a young civil rights activist*. New York: Atheneum Books for Young Readers.

Libenson, T. (2017). *Invisible Emmie*. New York: Penguin.

London, J. (1992). *Froggy gets dressed*. New York: Scholastic.

Lord, M. (2015). *A song for Cambodia*. New York: Lee & Low Books.

Lytle, C. (2019). *The infographic guide to American government*. New York: Adams Media.

Markel, M. (2013). *Brave girl: Clara and the shirtwaist makers' strike of 1909*. New York: HarperCollins.

Martin, J. B. (2009). *Snowflake Bentley*. New York: Houghton Mifflin.

Mass, W., & Stead, R. (2018). *Bob*. New York: Macmillan.

Morgan, E. (2014). *Next time you see the moon*. Arlington, VA: National Science Teacher Association Kids.

Morley, J. (n.d.). *You wouldn't want to be*. [series] New York: Franklin Watts.

Mortenson, G., & Roth, S. (2009). *Listen to the wind*. New York: Penguin.

Moss, M. (1995). *Amelia's notebook*. New York: Simon & Schuster.

Moss, M. (2013). *Barbed wire baseball*. New York: Abrams Books for Young Readers.

Mull, B. (2007). *Fabelhaven*. New York: Aladdin Paperbacks.

Munson, D. (2000). *Enemy pie*. New York: Chronicle Books.

Noble, T. H. (2007). *The orange shoes*. Ann Arbor, MI: Sleeping Bear Press.

O'Hearn, K. (2013). *The flame of Olympus*. New York: Aladdin Paperbacks.

Palacio, R. J. (2012). *Wonder*. New York: Knopf.

Palacio, R. J. (2019). *White bird*. New York: Knopf.

Pallotta, J. (n.d.). *Alphabet book*. [series] New York: Charlesbridge.

Pallotta, J. (n.d.). *Who would win*? [series] New York: Scholastic.

Pendergast, G. (2015). *The phases of the moon*. New York: Gareth Stevens.

Pilkey, D. (n.d.). *Captain Underpants*. [series] New York: Scholastic.

Pilkey, D. (2016). *Dogman*. New York: Scholastic.

Pulver, R. (2003). *Punctuation takes a vacation*. New York: Holiday House.

Rappaport, D. (2007). *Martin's big words*. New York: Hyperion Books for Children.

Rice, J. (1989). *Those mean, nasty, downright disgusting but invisible germs*. St. Paul, MN: Red Leaf Press.

Ringgold, F. (1991). *Tar beach*. New York: Crown.

Ringgold, F. (1992). *Aunt Harriet's Underground Railroad in the sky*. New York: Crown.

Ringgold, F. (1993). *If a bus could talk*. New York: Crown.

Ringgold, F. (1995). *My dream of Martin Luther King*. New York: Crown.

Ringgold, F. (2016). *We came to America*. New York: Aladdin.

Ryan, P. M. (2015). *Echo*. New York: Scholastic.

Santat, D., (2017). *After the fall*. New York: Roaring Brook Press.

Scholastic. (n.d.). Mexican migrant workers in the 20th century: Retrieved from *https://www.commonlit.org/en/texts/mexican-migrant-workers-in-the-20th-century*.

Schubert, I., & Schubert, D. (2011). *The umbrella*. Rotterdam, The Netherlands: Lemniscaat.

Sepahban, L. (2016). *Paper wishes*. New York: Farrar, Straus & Giroux.

Singer, M. (2011). *A full moon is rising*. New York: Lee & Low Books.

Smith, P. (2019). "They'll kill me if I'm sent back." Retrieved from: *https://junior.scholastic.com/issues/2018-19/012819/they-ll-kill-me-if-i-m-sent-back.html#970L*.

Spinelli, J. (1997). *The wringer*. New York: Scholastic.

Stanborough, R. (2020). *A women's suffrage time capsule: Artifacts of the movement for voting rights* (Time Capsule History). New York: Capstone Press.

Stanton, E. C. (1840). *Elizabeth Cady Stanton papers: Collection*. Retrieved from *www.loc.gov/collections/elizabeth-cady-stanton-papers/?fa=partof:elizabeth+cady+stanton+papers:+miscellany,+1840–1946*.

Stanton, T., & Blatch, H. S. (1922). *Elizabeth Cady Stanton as revealed in her letters, diary, and reminiscences*. Retrieved from *www.loc.gov/item/mss412100144*.

Sutherland, T. T. (2021). *The dangerous gift: Wings of fire*. New York: Scholastic Press.

Takei, G. (2019). *They called us enemy*. Marietta, GA: Top Shelf.

Tan, S. (2007). *The arrival*. New York: Levine Books.

Telgemeier, R. (2010). *Smile*. New York: Scholastic.

Thomson, B. (2010). *Chalk*. Las Vegas, NV: Amazon.

Tobin, P. (n.d.). *Plants vs. zombies*. [series] Milwaukie, OR: Dark Horse Books.

Tonatiuh, D. (2014). *Separate is never equal: Sylvia Mendez and her family's fight over desegregation*. New York: Abrams Books for Young Readers.

Tran, H., & Hackman, C. (2019). *Coming to America: A journey home*. New Providence, NJ: R. R. Bowker.

Vawter, V. (2014). *Paperboy*. New York: Yearling.

Warga, J. (2019). *Other words for home*. New York: Balzer Bray.

Warren, S. (2012). *Dolores Huerta: A hero to migrant workers*. Tarrytown, NY: Marshall Cavendish.

West, T. (1995). *Voyage of the Half Moon*. New York: Silver Moon Press.

Wiesner, D. (1991). *Tuesday*. New York: Clarion.

Wiesner, D. (2006). *Flotsam*. New York: Clarion.

Willems, M. (n.d.). *Elephant and Piggie*. [series] New York: Scholastic.

Willems, M. (n.d.). *Don't let the pigeon*. [series] New York: Scholastic.

Williams, K. L., & Mohammed, K. (2007). *Four feet, two sandals*. Grand Rapids, MI: Eerdmans.

Williams-Garcia, R. (2011). *One crazy summer*. New York: Quill Tree Books.

Winter, J. (2009). *Nasreen's secret school: A true story from Afghanistan*. San Diego, CA: Beach Lane Books.

Wolf, B. (2003). *Coming to America: A Muslim family's story*. New York: Lee & Low Books.

Woodson, J. (2016). *Brown girl dreaming*. New York: Puffin Books.

Yamada, K. (2013). *What do you do with an idea?* West Valley City, UT: Compendium.

Yousafzai, M. (2017). *Malala's magic pencil*. New York: Little, Brown Books for Young Readers.

Children's Literature by Appendix

APPENDIX A. BOOKS TO SUPPORT STUDENT AGENCY

Barnett, M. (2014). *Sam and Dave dig a hole*. Somerville, MA: Candlewick Press.
Bryant, J. (2013). *A splash of red: The life and art of Horace Pippin*. New York: Knopf Books for Young Readers.
Lewis, J., Ayden, A., & Powell, N. (2013). *March*. Marietta, GA: Topshelf.
Morales, Y. (2018). *Dreamers*. New York: Neal Porter Books.
Palacio, R. J. (2012). *Wonder*. New York: Knopf Books for Young Readers.
Reynolds, J. (2019). *Long way down*. New York: Atheneum/Caitlyn Dlouhy Books.
Vandever, D. W. (2017). *Fall in line, Holden*. Flagstaff, AZ: Salina Bookshelf.
Yousafzai, M., & Lamb, C. (2013). *I am Malala: The story of a girl who stood up for education and was shot by the Taliban*. London: Weidenfeld & Nicolson.

APPENDIX B. BOOKS TO TALK ABOUT VISIONING WITH STUDENTS

Alexander, K. (2018). *Rebound*. Boston: Houghton Mifflin Harcourt.
Archer, M. (2016). *Daniel finds a poem*. New York: Nancy Paulsen Books.
Jun, N. (2018). *My Beijing: Four stories of everyday wonder*. Minneapolis: Graphic Universe.
Mangal, M. (2018). *The vast wonder of the world: Biologist Ernest Everett Just*. Minneapolis: Millbrook.
Muñoz Ryan, P. (2015). *Echo*. New York: Scholastic.
Respicio, M. (2019). *The house that Lou built*. New York: Wendy Lamb Books.
Takei, G. (2019). *They called us enemy*. Marietta, GA: Top Shelf.

APPENDIX C. BOOKS BY GENRE

Folk Literature/Folktales/Fairytales

Belpre, P. (2004). *Perez y Martina*. New York: Penguin.
Hernandez, J. (2018). *The dragon slayer: Folktales from Latin America*. New York: Toon Graphics.

Norris, S. (2010). *Troy High*. New York: Abrams.

Slayton, S. (2018). *Cinderella's dress*. New York: Amaretto Press.

Science Fiction

Arnold, T. (n.d.). *Fly guy*. [series] New York: Scholastic.

Fox, H. (n.d.). *Eager*. [series] New York: Yearling.

Lowry, L. (1993). *The giver*. New York: Bantam Doubleday Dell.

Riordan, R. (n.d.). *Percy Jackson and the Olympians*. [series] New York: Hyperion Books for Children.

Biography/Autobiography

Barakat, I. (2016). *Tasting the sky: A Palestinian childhood*. New York: Farrar, Straus & Giroux.

Cook, M. (2012). *Our children can soar: A celebration of Rosa, Barack, and the pioneers of change*. New York: Bloomsbury.

Levy, D. (2016). *I dissent: Ruth Bader Ginsberg makes her mark*. New York: Simon & Schuster Books for Young Readers.

Robbins, S. J. (2018). *Malala: My story of standing up for girls' rights*. New York: Little, Brown.

Sweet, M. (2011). *Balloons over Broadway*. New York: Houghton Mifflin Books for Children.

Realistic Fiction

Draper, S. (2012). *Out of my mind*. New York: Atheneum Books for Young Readers.

Han, J. (2014). *Clara Lee and the apple pie dream*. New York: Hachette.

Lin, G. (2011). *Ling & Ting: Not exactly the same*. New York: Hachette.

Thomas, A. (2017). *The hate u give*. New York: Balzer + Bray.

Zimmer, T. V. (2007). *Reaching for the sun*. New York: Bloomsbury.

Historical Fiction

Anderson, L. H. (2010). *Chains*. New York: Atheneum Books for Young Readers.

Bruchac, J. (2006). *Code talker: A novel About the Navajo marines of World War Two*. New York: Dial Books.

Hess, K. (2004). *Cats in Krasinski Square*. New York: Scholastic.

Rappaport, D. (2007). *Martin's big words*. New York: Hyperion Books for Children.

Weatherford, C. B. (2016). *Freedom in Congo Square*. New York: Little Bee Books.

Graphic Novels

Craft, J. (2019). *New kid*. New York: Quill Tree Books.

Donkin, A., & Colfer, E. (2018). *Illegal*. Naperville, IL: Sourcebooks Jaberwocky.

Hatke, B. (series). (2014). *Zita the space girl*. New York: First Second.

Krosoczka, J. J. (series). (2012). *Lunch lady*. New York: Knopf Books for Young Readers.

Speigelman, A. (2013). *Jack and the box*. New York: Toon Graphics.

Poetry

Archer, J. M. (2016). *Daniel finds a poem*. New York: Nancy Paulsen Books.

Fogliano, J. (2016). *When green becomes tomatoes*. New York: Roaring Book Press.

Latham, I., & Waters, C. (2019). *Can I touch your hair? Poems of race, mistakes, and friendship*. Minneapolis: Carolrhoda Books.

Reynolds, J. (2019). *For everyone*. New York: Atheneum Books for Young Readers.

Narrative Nonfiction

Anderson, C. (2019). *We are not yet equal: Understanding our racial divide*. New York: Bloomsbury.

Fleischman, J. (2004). *Phineas Gage: A gruesome but true story about brain science*. Boston: Houghton Mifflin Harcourt.

Fleming, C. (2016). *Giant squid*. New York. Roaring Brook Press.

Expository

Aronson, M., & Budhos, M. (2017). *Robert Capa, Gerda Taro, and the invention of modern photojournalism*. New York: Macmillan.

Jenkins, S. (2014). *Eye to eye: How animals see the world*. Boston: Houghton Mifflin Harcourt.

Neri, G. (2018). *Grand theft horse*. New York: Lee & Low Books.

Turner, P. S. (2018). *Samurai rising: The epic life of Minamoto Yoshitsune*. Watertown, MA: Charlesbridge.

APPENDIX D. BOOK AWARDS

Acevedo, E. (2018). *The Poet X*. New York: Quill Tree Books.

Alexander, K. (2017). *Out of wonder: Poems celebrating poets*. Somerville, MA: Candlewick Press.

Bowles, D. (2018). *They call me Guero*. El Paso, TX: Cinco Puntos Press.

Daciūtė, E. (2018). *The fox on the swing*. London: Thames & Hudson.

Ewald, W. (2018). *America border culture dreamer: The young immigrant experience from A to Z*. New York: Little, Brown.

Hartfield, C. (2018). *A Few red drops: The Chicago race riots of 1919*. New York: Clarion Books.

Khorram, A. (2019). *Darius the great is not okay*. New York: Penguin.

Lê, M. (2018). *Drawn together*. New York: Little Brown Books for Young Readers.

Mangal, M. (2018). *The vast wonder of the world: Biologist Ernest Everett*. Minneapolis: Millbrook Press.

Maurer, T. (2017). *John Deere, that's who!* New York: Macmillan.

McAlister, C. (2017). *John Ronald's dragons: The story of J. R. R. Tolkien*. New York: Roaring Brook Press.

Mora, P. (2000). *Tomas and the library lady*. Decorah, IA: Dragonfly Books.

Morales, Y. (2018). *Dreamers*. New York: Neal Porter Books.

Myers, W. D. (2017). *Frederick Douglass: The lion who wrote history*. New York: Quill Tree Books.

Reynolds, J. (2019). *Long way down*. New York: Atheneum/Caitlyn Dlouhy Books/Simon & Schuster.

Rhodes, J. P. (2019). *Ghost boys*. New York: Little, Brown Books for Young Readers.

Ringtved, G. (2016). *Cry, heart, but never break*. Brooklyn, NY: Enchanted Lion Books.

Sanchez, E. (2019). *I am not your perfect Mexican daughter*. New York: Ember Books.

Sealaska Heritage Institute. (2017). *Shanyaak'utlaax: Salmon Boy*. Juneau, AK: Author.

Starr, A., & Boney, Jr., R. (2016). *Tales of the mighty code talkers: Volume one*. Albuquerque, NM: Native Realities.

Watson, R. (2018). *Piecing me together*. New York: Bloomsbury YA.

Wegelius, J. (2017). *The murderer's ape*. New York: Delacorte Press/Random House.

Yang, K. (2019). *Front desk*. New York: Scholastic.

Randolph Caldecott Medal

Blackall, S. (2018). *Hello lighthouse*. New York: Little, Brown Books For Young Readers.

Cordell, M. (2017). *Wolf in the snow*. New York: Feiwel & Friends.

Mattick, L. (2015). *Finding Winnie: The true story of the world's most famous bear*. New York: Hatchette Book Group.

Santat, D. (2014). *The adventures of Beekle: The unimaginary friend*. New York: Hatchette.

Steptoe, J. (2016). *Radiant child: The story of young artist Jean-Michel Basquiat*. New York: Little, Brown Books for Young Readers.

John Newbery Award

Alexander, K. (2014). *The crossover*. Boston: Houghton Mifflin Harcourt.

Barnhill, K. (2019). *The girl who drank the moon*. New York: Algonquin Readers.

de la Peña, M. (2015). *Last stop on Market Street*. New York: Putnam's.

Kelly, E. E. (2017). *Hello universe*. New York: Greenwillow Books.

Medina, M. (2018). *Merci Suárez changes gears*. Somerville, MA: Candlewick Press.

Orbis Pictus Award

Brown, D. (2017). *Drowned city: Hurricane Katrina & New Orleans*. Boston: Houghton Mifflin Harcourt.

Chin, J. (2017). *Grand Canyon*. New York: Roaring Brook Press.

Fleming, C. (2014). *The family Romanov: Murder, rebellion, & the fall of Imperial Russia*. Boston: Houghton Mifflin Harcourt.

Sweet, M. (2016). *Some writer!: The story of E. B. White*. Boston: Houghton Mifflin Harcourt.

Wallace, S. N. (2018). *Between the lines: How Ernie Barnes went from football field to the art gallery*. New York: Simon & Schuster.

APPENDIX E. POPULAR SERIES BOOKS

Bridwell, N. (2010). *Clifford*. New York: Cartwheel Books.

Brown, M. (2016). *Lola Levine*. New York: Little, Brown Books for Young Readers.

Collins, S. (2019). *Hunger games*. New York: Scholastic.

Dashner, J. (2010). *The Maze runner*. New York: Delacorte Press/Random House.

Dean, J., & Litwin, E. (2019). *Pete the cat*. New York: HarperCollins.

Griffiths, A., & Denton, T. (2016). *The treehouse books*. Stuttgart, Germany. Pan Macmillan.

Kibuishi, K. (2016). *Amulet*. New York: GRAPHIX.

Kinney, J. (2007). *Diary of a wimpy kid*. New York: Amulet

Krosoczka, J. (2009). *Lunch lady*. New York: Knopf Books for Young Readers.
May, K. (2013). *Lotus Lane*. New York: Scholastic.
McDonald, M. (2013). *Stink*. Somerville, MA: Candlewick Press.
Peirce, L. (2013). *Big Nate*. New York: HarperCollins.
Pilkey, D. (n.d.). *Captain Underpants*. [series] New York: Scholastic.
Riordan, R. (2011). *39 clues*. New York: Scholastic.
Riordan, R. (n.d.). *Percy Jackson and the Olympians*. [series] New York: Hyperion Books for
    Children.
Rowling, J. K. (2009). *Harry Potter*. New York: Levine Books.
Shusterman. H. (n.d.). *Arc of a scythe*. [series]. New York: Simon & Schuster Books for
    Young Readers.
Tarshis, L. (2019). *I survived*. New York: Scholastic.
Vernon, U. (2018). *Hamster princess*. New York, NY: Dial/Penguin.
Who Was/Where Was Series (2018). (various authors) New York: Penguin.
Willems, M. (n.d.). *Elephant and Piggie*. [series] New York: Scholastic.
Willems, M. (n.d.). *Don't let the pigeon*. [series] New York: Scholastic.

APPENDIX F. BOOK CLUB CHOICES

Elementary School Choices

Applegate, K. (2012). *The one and only Ivan*. New York: HarperCollins.
Bell, C. C. (2014). *El Deafo*. New York: Abrams.
Bradley, K. (2016). *The war that saved my life*. New York: Puffin Books.
Craft, J. (2019). *New kid*. New York: Quill Tree Books.
Gratz, A. (2017). *Refugee*. New York: Scholastic.
Meloy, M. (2013). *The apothecary*. New York: Puffin Books.

Young Adult Choices

Alexander, K. (2014). *The crossover*. Boston: Houghton Mifflin Harcourt.
Jackson, H. (2020). *A good girl's guide to murder*. New York: Delacorte Press/Random House.
La Sala, R. (2019). *Reverie*. Chicago: Sourcebooks Fire.
Palacio, R. J. (2019). *White bird*. New York: Knopf.
Takei, G. (2019). *They called us enemy*. Marietta, GA: Top Shelf.
Zusak, M. (2007). *The book thief*. New York: Knopf Books for Young Readers.

APPENDIX G. CHILDREN'S AND TEEN CHOICE BOOK AWARDS

Clements, A. (2018). *The losers club*. New York: Yearling.
Kane, J. (2018). *I say ooh you say aah*. London. Templar.
Lucile, T. (2017). *Poor Louie*. Somerville, MA: Candlewick Press.
Rhodes, J. P. (2019). *Ghost boys*. New York: Little, Brown Books for Young Readers.
Thomas, A. (2017). *The hate u give*. New York: Balzer + Bray.
Wagner, T. M. (2017). *Fifty wacky things animals do*. Lake Forest, CA: Walter Foster Jr.
Wang, J. (2018). *The prince and the dressmaker*. New York: First Second.
Zemeckis, R., & Gale. B. (2018). *Back to the future*. Philadelphia: Quirk Books.

Index

Note. *f* or *t* following a page number indicates a figure or a table.